EGER

The origins and development of the village of Egerton
and the activities of its principal families

Dimple School, Cox Green Road.

S. J. Tonge

Publication No 38

October 2019

No 38 Egerton
S J Tonge
Published by Turton Local History Society
October 2019
ISBN 978-1-904974-38-3

ACKNOWLEDGEMENTS

Sincere thanks are due to the people who have helped in the production of this booklet by sharing their knowledge and providing advice, especially Harry King and Peter Harris.

Photographs and maps credited to Bolton Archives and The Bolton News are reproduced with their permission.

For contributing photographs from their personal collections: Alison Ahmed, John Barlow, Anne Blackledge, Tom Carr, Phil Crabtree, Ruth Dover, John Hodgson, David Lloyd, David Livesey, Andy Robertson, Roderick Smith and Thirza Vickers.

Special thanks to Stephen Martin of Belmont, who contributed several photographs that were given to him by Jim Ingham, son of Bill Ingham, formerly the Deakins' gamekeeper, who lived in their shooting lodge (The Lords Hall) on Darwen Moor.

Photographs credited to Jason Wright are from a collection of previously unknown Ashworth family daguerreotypes purchased at auction in 2017, and conserved and digitised by Jason Wright. The original photographs are now in the possession of the National Gallery of Art Museum in Washington DC, USA.

The portrait of Henry Ashworth on page 38 is reproduced with the permission of the National Portrait Gallery, London. Detail from 'Henry Ashworth' by Samuel William Reynolds Jr, after Charles Allen Duval, mezzotint, published 1844.

TURTON LOCAL HISTORY SOCIETY

Turton Local History Society exists to promote an interest in history by discussion, research and record. It is particularly concerned with the history of the former Urban District of Turton and its constituent ancient townships of Bradshaw, Edgworth, Entwistle, Harwood, Longworth, Quarlton and Turton. Except for December, meetings are held from August to April inclusive, at 7:30pm on the fourth Wednesday of the month at Longsight Methodist Church Hall in Harwood. Visitors are welcome.

Previous publications are listed on the inside front cover. In recognition of the years of research undertaken and as a matter of courtesy and good academic practice, it is expected that due acknowledgment will be made to the author and Turton Local History Society when any further use is made of the content of this and previous publications.

CONTENTS

ILLUSTRATIONS

CHAPTER 1 INTRODUCTION

Prior to the 1830s, Egerton did not exist as the village we know today. It started to take shape after the turnpike road was built at the turn of the nineteenth century, and with the subsequent opening of Egerton Mill.

Formerly the area was predominantly isolated moorland in Turton, with a scattered collection of houses and farms. The community then was more spread out and fragmented, farmhouses stretching northwards up onto the hills towards Darwen, and over Longworth, on what is now open moorland.

Part of the area was the estate of the Walmsley family. A marriage in the seventeenth century between the stepdaughter of James Walmsley, and Ralph Egerton, brought the name Egerton to the area. The couple had no surviving sons, so the surname died out in Turton before it had even become established, but it survived in the name of their property, known as *Egerton's*.

During the industrial revolution, the property was acquired for building a textile mill. In its early days, the factory at Egerton earned a reputation for being well run and utilising the newest machinery. Its owners, the Ashworths, were well known for fair treatment of their operatives, and provision of favourable living and working conditions. Terraced stone cottages and other facilities were built for the increasing population, many of them mill workers, and the core of the current village came into being. With this expansion, the wider area became known as Egerton, which included not only Ralph Egerton's old estate, but also the surrounding properties at Dewhursts, Dimple, Dunscar, Stanrose and Stones.

Changes to the landscape of the village were slow over the next century or so, until the 1960s, when new housing developments significantly modified its character, and brought in an influx of new residents.

This booklet provides an overview of the history of Egerton, focusing on the lives of the families who gave their names to the area, and the businesses and activities of some of the principal families who contributed to its development.

CHAPTER 2   THE WALMSLEYS

Early Branches of the Walmsley Family

Egerton was formerly known by the name Walmsley, or simply the *'Higher End of Turton Township'*. Saxton's map of Lancashire from 1577 shows the chapels at Walmsley and Turton.

Local tradition is that the area was named Walmsley after the main landholders, and Walmsley Old Chapel was a domestic chapel built by the family at their own expense. The old chapel stood on Cox Green Road, near Egerton Community Primary School, the foundations of the eighteenth century rebuild still being visible.

The earliest records of the family name in Lancashire are in the thirteenth century, centred around Walmersley, now a suburban village, three miles north of Bury centre. From the late thirteen hundreds we find early branches of the family resident in Tockholes. By 1419, Roger de Walmersley was holding the Rogerstead estate in Heaton.

Saxton's 1577 Map of Lancashire showing Walmsley and Turton.

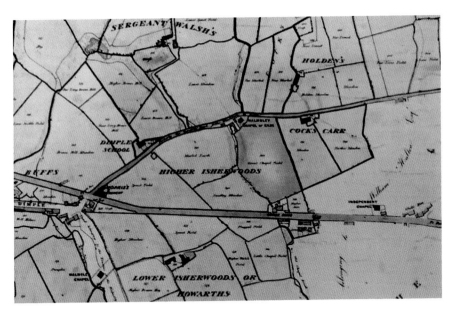

Walmsley Old Chapel highlighted in red, 'Great Chapel Field' highlighted in green (now Egerton C. P. School and Cox Green Close).
Part of a plan of land belonging to Peter R. Hoare in 1830 (Lancs. Archives).

Looking northwest towards Old Chapel House and surrounding fields in 1965.

Walmsley of Turton

The earliest record (so far found) of the Walmsley family in Turton is in 1407, when a marriage license was granted by the Archdeacon of Chester to Alice de Walmsley, and Richard son of William Thomasson of Turton. In the same year, Alice formally relinquished her property rights to Richard *Tomlinson* in a quitclaim deed, dated at Bolton.

Another early record is in the will of Sir James Harrington in 1493, which grants *'to Myles Worsley a mese in Turton in the holding of James Walmesley'* (*'mese'* short for messuage, an old term for a dwelling house with outbuildings and land). An inquisition at the death of his widow Isabella Harrington in 1520, showed that she held lands in various places including Turton, Blackrod and Longworth.

In 1560, we find a record of another James Walmsley, involved in a dispute with the lord of the manor of Turton. John Orrell of Turton Tower had enclosed two acres of moorland adjoining to his own land. His aggrieved tenants brought a case against him, Christopher Horrocks of Turton being their spokesperson. He complained that they had been deprived of their rights of pasture; that their livestock could no longer graze upon the land. The decision of the court is not known, but an outcome which satisfied the inhabitants evidently failed to arise. Two years later the land was still enclosed, and the angry tenants decided to do something about it. Twenty men armed with long pikes, staves, bows, arrows, swords, spades and short daggers, assembled at the enclosure and broke down the fences. Among those twenty men was one James Walmsley.

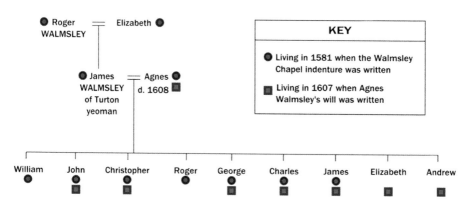

John Orrell seems to have been a domineering character and was frequently involved in lawsuits. A number of the Turton freeholders, including James Walmsley, banded together to try and protect themselves, agreeing to share the cost of any litigation against Orrell, and depositing their deeds together in a shared chest, for which four keys would be made, one for each of them.

After John Orrell died in 1581, his son William, the new lord of the manor, attempted to come to terms with the freeholders, to regain control of their interests in the land on Turton Moor, but it appears that the agreement was not endorsed by all parties, and may never have been finalised. In the same year, Walmsley had a legal document drawn up to try to ensure the succession of his estate to his wife and sons, the property being described as *'lands in Turton, then lately enclosed from the moor & half of Whalmsley Chapel Yard.'*

When Agnes, James Walmsley's widow, died in 1608, an inventory of her goods was made, which came to a value of over £31. This list of her possessions gives us a glimpse into their daily lives, showing that they kept farm animals, and processed wool for spinning. The inventory included, amongst other things, valuations for cows, sheep, hay, shears, cards and combs, wheels in the horse yard, an ark, four chests, pewter, brass and iron. Agnes' last will and testament stated that her body was to be buried at the parish church of Bolton, amongst her ancestors. She also gave ten shillings to the *'repaying'* of Walmsley Chapel, and twelve pence to *'lytele Annie Walmisley'* the daughter of James.

The Dealings of James Walmsley, Chetham's Steward

The last member of the principal land-holding branch of the Walmsley family in Turton was James Walmsley. His birth date is unknown, but would have been during the reign of Elizabeth I, probably in the 1570s. He may have been the son of James and Agnes Walmsley mentioned previously.

In 1604, James Walmsley married Katherine Kay at Bury, the daughter of Richard and Katherine Kay of Widdell (Woodhill) in Bury. They had a number of children, of whom two daughters survived: Anne and Elizabeth. Both were married when in their early twenties; Elizabeth to Christopher Horrocks of Turton at Walmsley Old Chapel in 1626, and Ann to Thomas Holme, gentleman, of Rochdale, in 1630.

Walmsley became one of the High Constables of the Hundred of Salford in 1620, along with James Chetham of Crumpsall, who was the older brother of Humphrey Chetham, later owner of the manor of Turton. Their first recorded duty was to collect a tax of twenty marks from the townships of the Hundred, to cover the costs of conveying people to the *'house of correction'*, where the idle, including vagrants and beggars, were set to work.

In 1626, Walmsley borrowed £200 from Humphrey Chetham, jointly with Francis Isherwood of Turton. He appears to have had Humphrey Chetham's confidence, and later started acting as his steward in estate affairs, corresponding on his behalf on business matters, and keeping accounts. He is variously described as Chetham's steward, factor and friend.

In 1628, Humphrey Chetham purchased the Turton estate from William Orrell, ending two centuries of Orrells as lords of the manor. A dispute later arose which shows that James Walmsley was involved in facilitating parts of the transaction. William Orrell's uncle Richard had originally agreed to resign his interest in the estate, and had paid James Walmsley £150 to ensure that William Orrell offered him good terms for doing so. After the mortgage to Chetham though, he changed his mind, and tried to make arrangements to clear part of the mortgage, and to allow the estate to descend into his family after William Orrell's death. The plan ultimately fell through, and Richard Orrell claimed that he had been defrauded out of the purchase of the Turton estate.

In addition to Chetham's business matters, and his own affairs in Turton, Walmsley was also branching out and taking interests further afield. Chetham was one of the wealthiest merchants in the northwest of England, and Walmsley's position as his steward may have allowed him to take advantage of opportunities that may not otherwise have befallen him. Unfortunately, it may have led him to extend beyond his means.

In 1641 Walmsley and three others entered into an agreement with John Preston of Furness to acquire mining rights to extract iron ore at Stainton with Adgarley (near Barrow-in-Furness), for six years, for a payment of £100. In the same year Walmsley jointly purchased the manors of Chipping and Goosnargh from Lord Strange (later 7th Earl of Derby), his associates being Hugh Cooper of Ormskirk, Thomas Wilson of Wrightington and James Whitaker of Manchester.

Following the death of his brother-in-law, Roger Kay, in 1637, Walmsley took responsibility for a fund that had been established for founding a school at Bury. The school's Board of Governors later alleged that he had used this money for himself. The legal proceedings in which they attempted to recover the money would continue to trouble his widow for decades after his death.

James Walmisley's signature, from a 1636 letter to George Chetham.

When his first wife died in 1643, James Walmsley married a widow, Elizabeth Robinson of Kearsley. Her late husband Ralph Robinson had been a wealthy man, and his daughters, Jane and Elizabeth, would become Walmsley's stepdaughters. Before getting remarried, he entered into an agreement with friends of the family acting as trustees for the stepdaughters, to determine what portions of their late father's estate belonged to the children, and to secure their marriage portions. Accordingly, he was paid £2,000, which he was later said to have used to pay some of his debts.

After the marriage, James Walmsley left Turton, and went to live in Kearsley. In 1648 he became sick, and while on his death-bed, debts appear to have caught up with him; the bailiffs arrived and seized his goods. Within a few days, and after some negotiation between the bailiffs and trustees acting for his stepdaughters, the debts were discharged.

He was buried on 13 January 1648 at Bolton. A will had been drawn up and signed only a week or so before his decease, and it was signed in the presence of some of his stepdaughters' trustees: William Blundell, Ellis Farnworth and Thomas Litherland, who seem to have been diligently fulfilling their duties in ensuring that the girls didn't lose out as a result of their mother having remarried. In the knowledge that there was not enough personal estate to honour the commitments made regarding his stepdaughters' entitlements, Walmsley conveyed property in Chipping and Kearsley to his wife as security for them. The Walmsley estate in Turton also ultimately came into their ownership.

The Last of the Walmsleys in Turton

The majority of James Walmsley's estate descended to his stepchildren and outside the direct Walmsley family, but other offshoots remained in Turton. In his will, James Walmsley left some very modest bequests to his cousins; *'George Walmesley my old cloak, and to his brother James Walmsley ten shillings'*. The term cousin was used fairly loosely and often meant nephew or niece.

In 1654, some members of the congregation of Walmsley Chapel (describing themselves as *'The godly in and about the Chapelry of Walmsley'*) sent a petition to Oliver Cromwell complaining that George Walmsley, Francis Isherwood, Thomas Kershaw, Roger Walkden and John Welsh had locked the chapel doors to prevent their minister Michael Briscoe from preaching. Later, Briscoe was ejected from Walmsley chapel because of his non-conformism.

In the hearth tax returns of 1666, George Walmsley was liable for three hearths. A date stone over the barn door of New Butterworth Farm, contains the initials G.W. and the date 1667. The date stone was said to be originally part of the old Butterworths Farm, which was located further up the hill, but no longer exists. A hint of the dwelling that used to be there can still be seen in the form of scattered stones and a solitary stone gatepost. Some sense of the former remoteness and isolation of the small community can be felt from Turton Heights, with a good view on a clear day over Bolton, Manchester and Winter Hill.

Andrew Walmsley, George's brother, went to Barbados, which had been settled by the English in 1625, and had become a wealthy sugar colony. He died there in 1674 and left a will, bequeathing goods to be shipped back to his brother George, who lived *'near Walmsley Chapel'*. Two years later, they had still not arrived. George's own will stated that they should be divided between his sons, *'if that legacie which my brother Andrew Walmesley hath given me come safe into England from Barbados'*. We might speculate that the cargo could have fallen victim to pirates in the Caribbean, who were active in this period.

The Walmsley family remained in Turton for a couple more generations. John, son of George Walmsley, leased land from Samuel Chetham in 1698. A house called *'Walmsleys'*, which has long since disappeared, can be found on the Ordnance Survey map in the 1840s, half a mile northeast from the old Butterworths Farm. Various records of the family can be found in parish registers, leases and manor court records, but not in any great numbers. By 1780, the land tax assessments show that nobody of the name Walmsley was recorded in Turton, as either owner, or occupier.

Date stone at New Butterworth Farm, off Cox Green Road 'GW 1667'.

Photograph from Blackburn Road in 1965 showing Cox Scar (centre), Old Globe and Old School (on the brow of the hill), prior to the building of Egerton CP School and the Druids Close and New Court Drive housing developments.

CHAPTER 3   THE EGERTONS

The Early History of the Egerton Family

The Egertons are an ancient Cheshire family who took the surname from the lordship of Egerton, an estate near Malpas in west Cheshire, which they acquired in medieval times. The current day civil parish of Egerton in Cheshire is still largely rural, and has a population of less than one hundred people.

In 1513 when Henry VIII invaded France, Ralph Egerton of Ridley was his standard-bearer, and was one of forty-nine *'valiant esquires'* who were knighted at Tournai Cathedral.

Sir Ralph Egerton's grandson, Sir Thomas Egerton (1540-1617), served as Lord Chancellor for twenty-one years, and was later 1st Baron Ellesmere and 1st Viscount Brackley. It is this Thomas Egerton that the public house at the centre of the village is named after (having previously been called The Globe up until 2006). The direct connection with the village however, is through the son of his half nephew, a less prominent offshoot of the family, of more modest means.

Sir Thomas Egerton's half nephew was Peter Egerton. In 1611, Peter married Elizabeth, the daughter and co-heir of Leonard Asshawe of Shaw Hall, near Flixton. Through this marriage, he became lord of Shaw and Flixton.

Peter Egerton was an active supporter of the parliament against Charles I. In 1641, he was appointed High Sheriff of Lancashire, and the following year took the Parliamentarian side and helped to organise the defence of Manchester against Royalist forces. In 1645, by then Colonel Egerton, he commanded 4,000 parliamentary troops at the 2nd Siege of Lathom House in Ormskirk, and was successful in accomplishing its downfall.

Peter's life was cut short in 1656, when he was accidentally poisoned. He was apparently suffering with some complaint, and sent the maid to the closet to mix flour of brimstone with milk, but in error she used mercury powder. He died within a few hours.

It was Peter's younger son, Ralph, who would later come to live in Turton, bringing the name Egerton to the place.

Sir Thomas Egerton
Viscount Brackley
1540 – 1617
Lord Chancellor
(Great uncle of
Ralph Egerton of Turton)

Mary Egerton, Lady Stanley
d. 1693
Wife to Sir Thomas Stanley
(sister of Ralph Egerton of Turton)
Portrait at Knowsley Hall,
nr. Liverpool

Thomas Egerton's signature
from around 1581.

Peter Egerton's signature
from a 1636 letter.

Ralph Egerton of Turton
signature from 1702.

𝕱𝖆𝖒𝖎𝖑𝖞 𝕿𝖗𝖊𝖊 of 𝕽𝖆𝖑𝖕𝖍 𝕰𝖌𝖊𝖗𝖙𝖔𝖓 of 𝕿𝖚𝖗𝖙𝖔𝖓

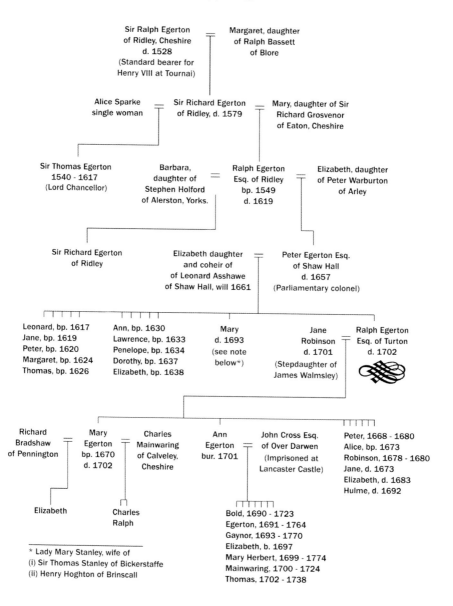

Sir Ralph Egerton — Margaret, daughter
of Ridley, Cheshire of Ralph Bassett
d. 1528 of Blore
(Standard bearer for
Henry VIII at Tournai)

Alice Sparke — Sir Richard Egerton — Mary, daughter of Sir
single woman of Ridley, d. 1579 Richard Grosvenor
of Eaton, Cheshire

Sir Thomas Egerton | Barbara, = Ralph Egerton | Elizabeth, daughter
1540 - 1617 daughter of Esq. of Ridley of Peter Warburton
(Lord Chancellor) Stephen Holford bp. 1549 of Arley
of Alerston, Yorks. d. 1619

Sir Richard Egerton | Elizabeth daughter = Peter Egerton Esq.
of Ridley and coheir of of Shaw Hall
of Leonard Asshawe d. 1657
of Shaw Hall, will 1661 (Parliamentary colonel)

Leonard, bp. 1617 | Ann, bp. 1630 | Mary | Jane | Ralph Egerton
Jane, bp. 1619 | Lawrence, bp. 1633 | d. 1693 | Robinson = Esq. of Turton
Peter, bp. 1620 | Penelope, bp. 1634 | (see note | d. 1701 | d. 1702
Margaret, bp. 1624 | Dorothy, bp. 1637 | below*) | (Stepdaughter of
Thomas, bp. 1626 | Elizabeth, bp. 1638 | | James Walmsley)

Richard | Mary = Charles | Ann = John Cross Esq. | Peter, 1668 - 1680
Bradshaw = Egerton Mainwaring Egerton of Over Darwen | Alice, bp. 1673
of Pennington bp. 1670 of Calveley, bur. 1701 (Imprisoned at | Robinson, 1678 - 1680
d. 1702 Cheshire Lancaster Castle) | Jane, d. 1673
| Elizabeth, d. 1683
| Hulme, d. 1692

Elizabeth | Charles | Bold, 1690 - 1723
Ralph | Egerton, 1691 - 1764
Gaynor, 1693 - 1770
Elizabeth, b. 1697
Mary Herbert, 1699 - 1774
Mainwaring, 1700 - 1724
Thomas, 1702 - 1738

* Lady Mary Stanley, wife of
(i) Sir Thomas Stanley of Bickerstaffe
(ii) Henry Hoghton of Brinscall

Ralph Egerton, Esq. of Turton

Ralph Egerton was a younger son of Peter and Elizabeth Egerton of Shaw Hall, Flixton. His baptism record has not survived, but it would likely have been at the church of St. Michael in Flixton, like the majority of his siblings, between 1620 and 1640.

Ralph's brother Leonard, as eldest son, would inherit the family estate at Shaw Hall. Their sisters were matched with husbands from wealthy families. Mary married twice, firstly to Sir Thomas Stanley of Bickerstaffe, 2nd baronet, and secondly to Henry Hoghton of Brinscall (grandson of Sir Richard Hoghton of Hoghton Tower). Jane married Edmund Lathom of Irlam, and Dorothy married Thomas Holcroft of Hurst.

In 1663, Ralph married Jane Robinson of Kearsley, stepdaughter of James Walmsley of Turton. Shortly after 1668, they moved to the old Walmsley estate at Turton, which afterwards became known as Egerton's.

The location of the house, the old seat of the Walmsley family, was around the area that is now Egerton Park and the Egerton House Hotel. On the 1797 turnpike map it was named as *'Egerton Hall'*, but was later known as *'Egerton Old Hall'* to avoid confusion with the home of Edmund Ashworth, built in the 1820s on the opposite side of Blackburn Road.

'Egerton Old Hall' appears to have been a substantial and well-furnished house. It included a brewhouse, kitchen, parlour, hall, buttery, larder, dairy, closet, little room and eight chamber rooms. In the hearth tax returns of 1666, Mrs. Walmsley's house had six hearths, second only to Turton Tower in the township which had fourteen (comparing with other local manor houses such as Hall i'th' Wood which also had six, and Entwistle Hall which had seven). An inventory of Ralph Egerton's goods was compiled in 1702, which catalogues the contents of the hall, and helps us to get a sense of how it may have looked (Appendix B).

Following in his father's military footsteps, Ralph served in the militia during the 1670s, being a lieutenant of horse, and also acting as treasurer.

Ralph and Jane Egerton had eight children between 1670 and 1683; Mary, Alice, Robinson, Jane, Peter, Elizabeth, Ann and Hulme. At least four of them died in infancy and were buried at Bolton parish church *'intra ecclesiam'*, inside the church building rather than in the churchyard, as to be expected for a family of their standing.

Egerton Barn Cottage in 2019.

Originally known as Egerton Farm, Egerton Barn Cottage was said to have been built partly with stone reused from Egerton Old Hall, following its demolition in the 1830s.

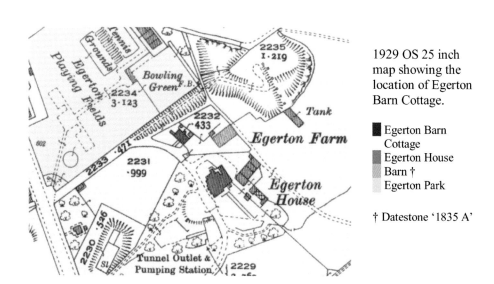

1929 OS 25 inch map showing the location of Egerton Barn Cottage.

▉ Egerton Barn Cottage
▉ Egerton House
▨ Barn †
▢ Egerton Park

† Datestone '1835 A'

Son-in-Law Trouble

In 1689, Ralph's daughter Ann married John Crosse, son of William Crosse of Upper Darwen. As part of the marriage settlement, Ralph paid £200 to his new son-in-law and £350 to his father, on the understanding that after their deaths, the Crosse family estates at Upper Darwen Hall (also known as Liveseys) and Turncroft would be settled on any children from the marriage. They also made provision for the maintenance of any children should their parents die, of £5 a year for each child.

Between 1690 and 1700, John and Ann Crosse had four sons and three daughters; Bold, Gaynor, Egerton, Elizabeth, Mainwaring, Mary and Thomas.

Ralph & Jane Egerton did not appear to have much confidence in their new son-in-law's ability to manage his financial affairs. They were concerned that he would encumber the Crosse estates with debt, be unable to maintain his wife and children, and endanger their inheritance. In 1692, they had him enter into a bond for £400, in which he guaranteed a £20 annuity to be paid to their daughter Ann for her maintenance, and, later, another agreement to further protect the estate from encumbrances. John Crosse subsequently failed to pay the annuity, and proved his in-laws right, by falling into debt, resulting in a warrant being issued for his arrest.

When the bailiffs came to Turton to detain him, he evidently put up a struggle. Hearing the commotion from a distance, two day-labourers named Lawrence Fielding and Anthony Ormeroyd, who were working for Mr. Crosse on that day, came to his aid, and rescued him. They later had to answer at the Quarter Sessions for obstructing the constables in their duties. Despite the trouble they made for themselves, Mr. Crosse did not long remain free, and was subsequently imprisoned at Lancaster Castle.

While John Crosse was in prison, his wife Ann died in 1701, leaving six children all under twelve years old. He later alleged that, following the death of his wife, her parents had gone to the hall at Upper Darwen, and had taken clothes, rings, jewels and other valuables belonging to her, as well as some of his own belongings. They were also alleged to have taken various deeds and papers relating to the Crosse family estates, and subsequently 'received the rents and profits thereof'.

In 1701, Ralph's wife Jane died, and he a year later. The decline in his health appears to have come fairly quickly; he signed Letters of Administration for his late wife's estate in July 1702, in a fairly strong and clear hand, yet within two months he had only the strength to sign his own last will and testament with a cross. He died within a month.

Executor's Expenses Accounts

Ralph Egerton's funeral was on 7th October 1702. The following items are selected entries from John Barlowe & Charles Beswick's expenses accounts, relating to events around the time of Ralph's death, and his funeral.

Item	Cost
Sent Mr. Cross Senr. by Robt. Fielden a Servant to Mr. Egerton 10. and to acquaint him of Mr. Egerton his father in Laws death	£0:10s:0d
pd. for Carridge of Letters to Lancaster and back and to Mr. Cross Children at Blackburn	£0:1s:0d
Paid Mr Kenyon for Crape* for the funeral	£2:2s:3d
To Jno. Howarth for Coffin	£1:2s:0d
to John Ogden for Cloth to Cover the Coffin	£0:9s:2d
To the Collectors for buriall the Deceased being an Esqr	£5:0s:0d
pd. Pason Stones for Mr. Egerton's funerall sermon 10 and to the Ringers 6	£0:16s:0d
Paid Abraham Ogden for Shopp goods for the funerall	£4:0s:0d
Paid for wine, sack, Piggs etc.	£0:15s:5d
Paid Edmund Greenhalgh for meat & drink at Mr. Egerton's funerall	£4:10s:0d
Paid Mr. Hulton's Servts. for Coach bottom	£0:15s:0d
for Vinegar-Capers & other odd things	£0:1s:7d
for Veal, Mutton & Tobacco & carriage	£0:5s:2d
to James Hardman of Bolton for Ale	£2:1s:8d
to Charles Holland for Ale	£1:13s:0d
to Mr. Hadden for Mortuary	£0:10s:0d
to Henry Wilkinson for wine	£0:15s:5d
John Wood for Grass for Mr. Egerton's gray horse	£0:19s:6d
Paid tyth & Lords rent to Mr. Chetham's Steward	£0:12s:6d

Three sale days of Goods at Turton 27th, 28th, 29th of October 1702

* Black silk / fabric, formerly used for mourning clothes.

CHAPTER 4   THE CROSSES

Legal Disputes Following Ralph Egerton's Death

Ralph Egerton left a will, in which he claimed possession of lands in Flixton, Chipping, Hoddlesden, Turton, Darwen and Pennington. An inventory of his goods was valued at £205 18s 0½d, and his debtors owed him £761. He appointed James Kay of Heap, James Barlow of the same, yeoman, and Charles Beswick of Manchester, as the executors. Their administration of the will would later be called in to question, and the Barlow family in particular would come to rue the day that James Barlow agreed to act.

The executors went to Blackburn to visit the Egertons' grandchildren, the Crosse children, paying for their clothes and schoolbooks. Mary Edge, who had been the Egertons' housekeeper, repaired the children's clothes and paid board money to their schoolmaster. The executors also arranged for *'Old Mr. Crosse'* to receive the £15 a year allowance granted under the will, sending it up to Lancaster Castle, along with any clothing he requested.

John Crosse recovered possession of the estate at Turncroft following his release from Lancaster Castle, and his son Bold purchased the interest in it from him. Bold reached the age of twenty-one on 8 Feb 1710, and should then have been entitled to £100 from his grandfather's estate, but this was not paid. He claimed that he had to borrow money at interest to make provision for the maintenance of his brothers and sisters who otherwise might have starved, or had to be maintained by the parish overseers.

In 1719, the Crosse family exhibited a bill in the Court of Chancery, attempting to get to the truth of where their family's wealth had gone, and to recover some of it. They accused the executors of falsifying the accounts of Ralph Egerton's estate, of concealing debts that they themselves owed him, of pretending that Egerton had himself been in debt, and of submitting fictitious expenses. They demanded to be given information about the disbursement of their grandparents' assets, and those of their great grandmother Elizabeth Walmsley, and great aunt Elizabeth Hulme.

The executors certified that they *'did never intermeddle nor had in their possession.... any of the Goods of the above said Ralph Egerton, nor doe they know of any papers or other matter relating to him the said Ralph Egerton.'* Elizabeth Barlow spoke on behalf of James Barlow, one of the original executors, who had by then died. This was not to be the last time that the Barlow family would tangle with the Crosses.

Accusations of Skullduggery against Mary Herbert Crosse

Bold Crosse of Over Darwen died in 1723 aged 33. In his will he left his *'messuage and Tenement with the Appurts in Turton in the said County, Commonly called or known by the name Egertons'*, to John Walmsley the younger of Wigan, along with land in Flixton formerly belonging to his grandfather. He left instructions that the estate should be sold to satisfy any just debts that he had at the time of his decease. It appears however, to have descended into the possession of one of his younger sisters, Mary Herbert Crosse.

She was twenty-four years old when her eldest brother, Bold, died. A year after his death, she was granted probate of their great grandmother's estate, declaring herself as the next of kin. Elizabeth Walmsley had at that point been dead for nearly half a century, but portions of her estate had evidently been left unadministered by her children.

By 1737, we know that Mary Herbert was in possession of Egertons, because she was fined for four years in a row for failing to serve on the jury at the Turton court leet.

She appears to have pursued her property interests forcefully, going to court to try to recover income from estates in Rivington, to which she claimed entitlement. Her tactics in other transactions seem to have been questionable. She was alleged to have tricked her sister, Gaynor, into selling her share of a property in Flixton, and then, once in possession, refused to pay for it. This modus operandi was later used again, as we see from the following warning notice in the newspaper, Whitworth's Manchester Magazine, published on 16 June 1741:

This is to give Notice,

TO any one that lends Money upon Mortgage, or Buys from *Mrs. Mary Herbert Croffe*, of *Turton*, in the Parifh of *Bolton le Moors*, and the County of *Lancafter*, the Eftate of Mr. *John Barlow* and his *Brothers*, late of *Water* in the Parifh of *Bury*, and County of *Lancafter*, which Eftate all lies in the Parifh of *Bury* and County of *Lancafter*, may depend upon immediate Trouble in the Law, She having got into it, as Mr. *Barlow* fays, by a Clandeftine Method, and not having paid one half-penny Confideration Money for it.

In 1744, by then in her mid-forties, she married Abel Flitcroft of Manchester, and he came to live with her at Egertons. Mr Flitcroft served as overseer of the highway, as a juror at Turton court leet, and was also recorded in some disputes with neighbours and for a minor misdemeanor, having let his horse run dangerously on the highway. They stayed for a decade or so at Egertons, before moving away.

Thomas Fogg then occupied Egertons and paid the chief-rent for it. Mary Herbert must have retained ownership of it until her death in 1774, as it then came into the possession of her nephew, the only surviving son of her brother Thomas. The new owner was Egerton Crosse of Kearsley Hall, a major of the Royal Lancashire militia.

The End of the Crosse Line

In 1787, a personal letter from Adam Lomax, a solicitor of Dunscar, to his old friend Rev Edward Walmsley, lamented the dilapidated state of the old hall at Egertons, *'formerly the estate of your reputable family'*. About it, he said that it was *'now in ruins, to the great scandal of the present owner and no good to the tenants. I have often viewed the place with surprise to see the ruins of the Walmsley seat.'* Lomax's letter speaks highly of the *'ancient worthy'* Walmsley family, but he thought that the Crosses were *'of little worth'*.

Major Crosse died in 1803, leaving equal shares in the Egertons estate to his wife Ellen, and spinster sister Ann, who themselves died in 1810 and 1814 respectively. On the 6th June 1814, at four o'clock in the afternoon, an auction was held at the Bridge Inn in Bolton, to dispose of the estate. It comprised five lots, including estates in Bury, Kearsley, thirty-six acres at Turton, and rights to a pew at Ringley Chapel.

With the sale, the property passed out of the hands of the descendants of the old Egerton family of Turton. The Egerton family's association with the area that eventually became known by their name was relatively short lived; Ralph Egerton only actually lived in Turton for about thirty-two years. By 1842, Egerton Old Hall had been pulled down, and its remains converted into a cottage.

Land Tax Records for Egertons in Turton (1780 – 1830)

Years Between	Proprietor	Occupier
1780 - 1783	Egerton Cross, Esq.	Thomas Kershaw
1786 - 1789		Thomas Bridge
1790 - 1801		William Haslam & others
1802 - 1811	Egerton Cross, Esq. (widow)	James Rothwell & others
1812 - 1815		Nuttall family
1816 - 1823	William Balshaw	
1824 - 1825		John Orrell
1826	Philip Novelli	Jane Bridge
1827 - 1828	Philip Novelli & Co.	Novelli & Bodmer
1829 - 1830	Henry Ashworth & Co.	Henry Ashworth & Co.

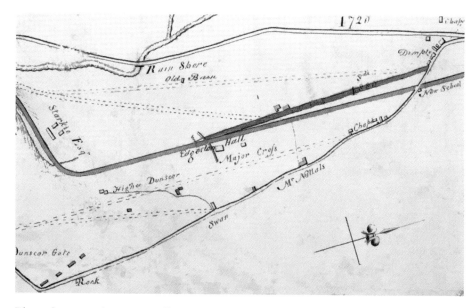

Plan of proposed new turnpike road c1796 (Bolton Archives ref: ZAL1358). Note *Edgerton Hall* in the centre, owned by *Major Cross*. The building owned by *Starkie Esq* is Mather Fold (near the present day war memorial), *Mr Nuttals* became known as Old Globe (on Cox Green Road). *New School* is Dimple School.

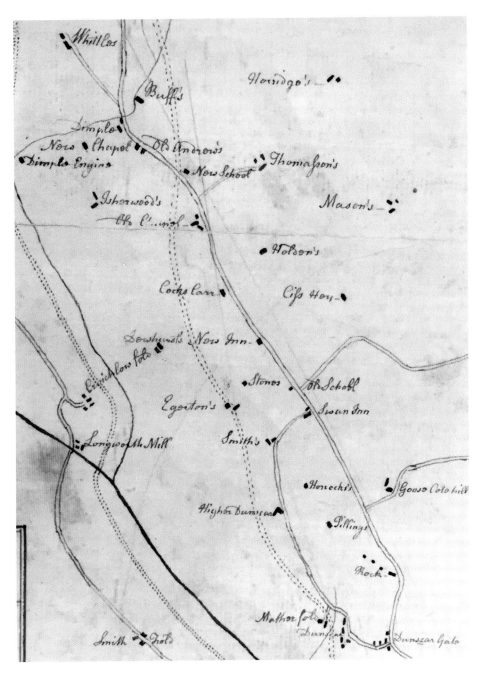

Plan for proposed new turnpike road c1795 (Bolton Archives ref: ZAL1342).

21

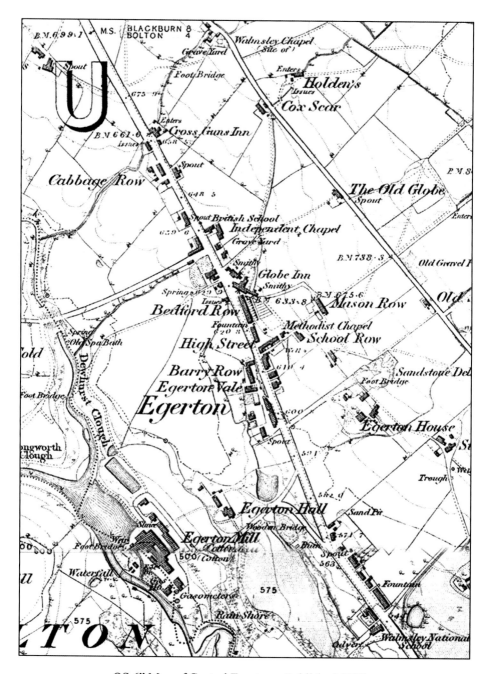

OS 6" Map of Central Egerton – Published 1850.

22

CHAPTER 5   THE BUILDING OF EGERTON

Migration from the Old Highway to the New Road

(Cox Green Road & Blackburn Road)

By 1800, the Bolton & Blackburn turnpike road had started to organise the area into a shape we would recognise today. Previously the main road had been Cox Green Road, known locally within living memory as *'the old road'*. The place that is now the centre of Egerton was then mainly farmland and meadows with a few scattered cottages, farmhouses and pathways.

Throughout the eighteenth century, the manor court of Turton enforced road maintenance – ensuring the tenants were looking after the sections of road that abutted their properties; building fences and walls, cutting back hedges and digging ditches to allow proper drainage. Anyone who has walked along Cox Green Road after heavy rain will have seen the water running down from the hills and flowing down the drainage channel, and it is easy to imagine how the condition of the old road could have quickly deteriorated without proper upkeep.

There are a number of records in the manor court books of proceedings relating to the old road, of which a few examples follow. In 1761, six people were fined for allowing water from their land to run onto the road, between Walmsley Chapel and the Smithy. In 1778 the blacksmith John Kay, was fined for not removing rubbish from the highway, and again for not re-erecting a wall having got stone for a building at Stanrose (probably Old Swan Cottages that carries a date stone *'John & Alice Kay 1778'*). The following year, sixteen local residents were fined two shillings each for failing to maintain a stretch of wall from Little Stanrose to Great Stanrose, between the meetings of Cox Green Road and the present day roads Great Stone Close and New Court Drive.

A newspaper correspondent for the Bolton Evening News traced the route of the old road in 1878, and gave the following account:

'...leading to the high ground and semi-mountain road past Cox Green stone quarries, with the hill or eminence known as 'Cheetham's Close' on the right, and the village of Egerton to the left. As the road gets more on the level there are four stacks of buildings on the left, at varying distances apart. The first approached formerly a roadside 'public', called the 'Swan', with the date 1778 over the doorway; next called the old school, next again, formerly a roadside 'public' known as the old 'Globe'. The fourth a farm house, and about 100 yards from the last point are to be seen, in a small oblong enclosure over shadowed by trees, the base and all that now popularly remains of Walmsley old Episcopalian chapel.'

Cox Scar farm in the foreground, looking southeast up
Cox Green Road towards the Old Globe taken in the 1960s.

Old Globe on Cox Green Road (centre).
(both pictures from Robert Walch Collection – TLHS archives).

Old Swan cottages on Cox Green Road in the 1960s (Bolton News).
Date stone *'John & Alice Kay 1778'*.

Dimple School, Cox Green Road, built 1795.

Bolton & Blackburn Turnpike Road

By 1787, businessmen from Blackburn became interested in improving the road between Bolton and Blackburn, and in establishing a turnpike trust to construct and manage it. They gave notice in the Manchester Mercury of a meeting at the Black Bull public house in Blackburn on 28 August, to consult with interested parties. There they resolved to apply to Parliament, and scheduled another meeting at the same place two weeks later inviting *'all persons inclined to promote such undertaking'*. Again, they advertised the meeting in the Manchester Mercury, and put up notices in the affected townships.

It seems there was resistance to the idea, and meetings were organised at Over Darwen, Lower Darwen and Turton to prevent the plan from going forward. Mrs Mary Greene, lady of the manor of Turton, asked her attorney Mr Ridgway of Manchester to attend the meeting at Blackburn in her stead, and George Hargreaves of Haslingden, appealed to James Brandwood to organise local opposition. At a meeting of landowners and inhabitants of Turton, it was unanimously agreed that a turnpike road was not needed as the current road was of proper construction and in good repair. They raised concerns that a toll road would be 'oppressive' to local inhabitants, particularly the poor, who would have to pay a toll to carry their coal. Forty-four Turtoners signed a statement opposing the proposal.

Undeterred, the promoters of the plan continued, drawing up a draft bill for Parliament and arranging further meetings at Blackburn in December 1787, but after this the project appears to have been dropped.

Parliament was by this point passing hundreds of acts a year establishing new turnpikes, significantly strengthening the country's road capacity. Ten years after the original plan was abandoned, a new one was drawn up, which followed the line of Blackburn Road as we know it today. The Act was passed allowing the creation of the trust, with two hundred and thirty-three trustees, including at least thirteen of the people who had objected previously. The trustees included Egerton Crosse, the Reverend James Folds (incumbent of Walmsley Chapel), Ely Gledhill, Edmund Haworth, the Reverend Amos Ogden, the Reverend Richard Rothwell (of Sharples Hall, owner of the Dunscar estate), as well as rising local industrialists like the Ashworths, Ainsworths and Knowles families.

The landowners wasted no time in taking advantage of the new road link. Even as it was still under construction, they started advertising in the newspaper to let out hundreds of acres of land in Over Darwen to colliers, for whom transport of the coal they produced would now be considerably easier. More evidence of the road being built can be seen in September 1797, when a notice appeared in the newspaper inviting contractors to tender for building a new bridge over Cadshaw Brook, at a meeting at John Nuttall's, the sign of the Globe, in Turton.

John Nuttall was the innkeeper at the Globe, and a landowner. He had acquired the northeast portion of the Dewhurst estate from the Dewhurst family sometime around 1795, and also built the original Globe Inn around the same time, on Cox Green Road. Soon after the new road was completed, Nuttall built the new Globe Inn, the previous building being then called Old Globe Inn or Higher Globe Inn.

Similarly, the Cross Guns relocated from the old road to the new road. By 1873 the old Cross Guns, which stood on the old road next to the chapel, was said to be a *'cold and comfortless'* ruin, and by 1890 it had disappeared from the map. Walmsley old chapel itself was demolished in the 1830s, and replaced by Christ Church Walmsley, about a mile away, on the new road.

The new road and the migration down the hill of the local inns, smithies, and chapel caused a rearrangement of the area. Local farmers and landowners started to build cottages on either side of the new road. One example is the row of cottages on Blackburn Road, now numbered 309 to 315. In 1807, John Nuttall leased some of his land to the Globe Inn's Male & Female Friendly Societies; sections of fields called Nearer Calf Hey and Further Calf Hey were fenced off for building (the remainder later became Egerton Cricket Club). The two Friendly Societies built two cottages each on the land, the rental income from which went into the societies' coffers to be used to support their members in times of sickness or hardship.

John Nuttall died in 1812, and left the business and premises to his wife Patty. She ran a multitude of businesses and seems to have been an industrious and enterprising woman. A series of very personal letters written in 1814 and 1815 between Patty and her son John (and other family members) have survived, and give an intimate insight into their family relationships, and some idea of their business activities. As well as running the inn, Patty was overseeing the planting and harvesting of crops of wheat, potatoes and turnips on their land (nine fields between Cox Green Road down to the bottom of what is now the cricket field).

In 1823 Patty put the inn and land up for sale with a notice in the Bolton Express, describing it as a *'well accustomed Inn and Public House known by the sign of the Globe with the back kitchen, stable, brewhouse, garden and yard adjoining thereto.'* The estate was divided into four lots, and appears to have been sold in pieces, after which the Nuttalls moved to Bolton.

A procession heading south past The Globe, thought to be in the early 1900s.

The Globe pictured in the 1960s (Bolton News).

PLAN OF THE ESTATE BELONGING TO THE LATE JOHN NUTTALL c1824

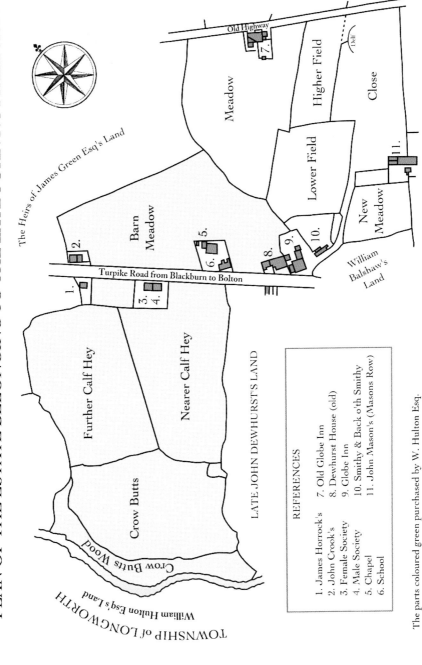

The Heirs of James Green Esq's Land

Old Highway

7.

Meadow

Delf

Higher Field

Close

Mr George Warburton's Land

Barn Meadow

2.

5.

6.

Lower Field

8.

9.

11.

New Meadow

10.

William Balshaw's Land

Turpike Road from Blackburn to Bolton

1.

3.
4.

Further Calf Hey

Nearer Calf Hey

Crow Butts

Crow Butts Wood

William Hulton Esq's Land

TOWNSHIP of LONGWORTH

LATE JOHN DEWHURST'S LAND

REFERENCES

1. James Horrock's
2. John Crook's
3. Female Society
4. Male Society
5. Chapel
6. School
7. Old Globe Inn
8. Dewhurst House (old)
9. Globe Inn
10. Smithy & Back o'th Smithy
11. John Mason's (Masons Row)

The parts coloured green purchased by W. Hulton Esq.
c1824. Based on plan at Lancashire Archives, ref: DDHU/ACC8410/245

Numbers 309 to 315 Blackburn Road pictured in 2007.
These cottages were built around 1807 by the Friendly Societies of The Globe.

Cottages on Blackburn Road, Albert Street and Taylor's Terrace.

Longworth Road

William Hulton Esquire purchased a large part of the Nuttalls' land, presumably to link his estate in Longworth with the turnpike road. He was a wealthy landowner and magistrate, known for having dealt harshly with the Luddites for arson at Westhoughton Mill in 1814 - four of them being hanged at Lancaster Castle. He was also notorious for the part he played in the 1819 Peterloo Massacre in Manchester, having ordered the cavalry to disperse the crowds, causing fifteen deaths and many injuries.

In 1830, William Hulton had plans drawn up for Longworth New Road, running from Blackburn Road to Critchley Fold, joining the old lane to Longworth Hall. Tenders were submitted, and the work was awarded to three local stonemasons; Thomas Marsh, Samuel Helme and Thomas Taylor, for the price of £560. They were given seven months to build the road, but failed to hit the deadline, and signed the contract over to John Harrison, a labourer, to finish it off.

This section of Longworth Road was built in 1831-32 on William Hulton's land, linking the Bolton & Blackburn turnpike to Longworth.

The Beginnings of Industry in Egerton

In 1826, the Egertons estate was bought by a consortium of business men, financed by Philip Novelli, an Italian merchant living in Manchester. His partners were Johann Georg Bodmer, a Swiss engineer, and an otherwise unknown Swiss chemist, and their intention was to build a cotton mill and dye-works.

Bodmer was a prolific inventor who had patented an invention for cotton manufacturing which made the process from carding to spinning a continuous one. He came to 'Cottonopolis' Manchester, and was advised by friends to prove the superiority of his invention by exhibiting the machines at work in a mill. Around 1826, Bodmer moved to Turton, and erected a small building near Merry Cock Hall. Into the building, he fitted his recently patented machines, not to carry on a manufacturing business, but as a showroom to demonstrate his inventions to local manufacturers. He is said to have planted mulberry trees, presumably with a view to introducing silkworms.

Bodmer went into partnership with Novelli and the pair identified Egertons as a suitable site for a mill, and accordingly acquired it, Novelli providing the finance. Bodmer went to reside there during construction, in a temporary building, composed of bricks and planks, a short distance from where Egerton Mill was being built.

After two years, having spent £40,000, and with the mill still not in production, Novelli refused go any further with the venture. Work on the mill was stopped and it was offered for sale. Some accounts state that Bodmer's health was failing and he therefore returned to Switzerland, but an 1829 letter from him to Henry Ashworth sheds more light on the reasons for his decision to walk away from Egerton:

'..it was certainly my wish to be proprietor of Egerton and had some hopes that things might be arranged to my satisfaction. I would have liked to finish the works I had begun, I was determined in that case to give up all scheeming [inventing] *and to turn manufacturer, but my children, though they would have followed me anywhere, declared most positively that they would rather have but little in their own country, than a large fortune in England. My son George who, by the by, turned out a capital young man, will pursue his studies, and Rodolphe, though he shows inclination for engineering is young and may perhaps prefer following another business, so that for all my trouble I would have been left alone at Egerton, and I would have had once more a very heavy load upon my shoulders, without prospects of doing any good for my children.*

I was however returned to Paris, where I received a letter from Zurich from my children and brothers and of some of my friends in France, who all advised me not to undertake so heavy a concern, and a letter of Mr Trumplers, wrote by Mr Novelli's order, that besides those £12,000 and the materials &c. I would have to pay £5,000 more in case I should take Egerton, though this last sum was not clearly mentioned in the letter Mr Novelli gave me before I left England. All those circumstances determined me to give up at once the idea of doing any more steps for this business and though it was very mortifying at first, I have had reason enough ever since to thank God, that it could not be as I wished it at that time.'

After his death in 1864, The Institution of Civil Engineers published a thirty-five page memoir about Bodmer's life and achievements, including six pages describing his inventions, which were covered in his thirteen patents between 1834 and 1844.

Johann Georg Bodmer (1786 – 1864)
Commemorative stamp released in 1964 in Switzerland.

Merry Cock Hall in the 1950s, looking north up Blackburn Road.

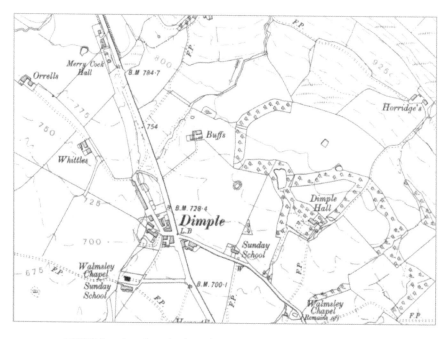

1908 Map showing the location of Merry Cock Hall (top left).

Merry Cock Hall - demolished in 1960.

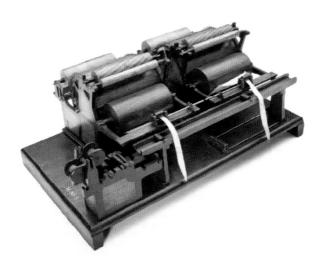

Model of Bodmer's carding engine, 1820 – 1824.
Science Museum Group Collection Online.

CHAPTER 6   THE ASHWORTHS

Egerton Mill

Walmsley was put on the map by the Walmsley family and their chapel; Ralph Egerton gave his name to the estate; Bodmer was the engineer and inventor who planted the seeds of industry; but it is the Ashworths who brought those plans to fruition, and who must be given much of the credit for moulding the village of Egerton as we know it today.

The Ashworths' business activities have been well documented by Rhodes Boyson, in his book *The Ashworth Cotton Enterprise* (1970). It is essential reading for anyone who is interested in Egerton.

The Ashworth family had settled at the Oaks farms in Turton during the seventeenth century, and soon after also acquired Birtenshaw farm. Originally yeoman farmers, later generations began to specialise in textiles. John Ashworth (1772-1855) built New Eagley Mill in the 1790s, and was soon afterwards joined by his brother Edmund as a business partner. Their modestly sized mill was never particularly profitable, and often a liability. The Ashworth brothers had a number of business interests, and the mill did not have the full focus of their attention.

Two of John's sons, Henry and Edmund, joined the family business and were given quarter shares in the profits. Their father and uncle remained as partners while also attending to their other interests, but for the two newcomers it was their only source of income and primary focus. Over the coming years, they expanded the mill, invested in machinery, and improved working practices. With their ambition, energy, and persistent attention to detail, they began to transform the mill into one that was efficiently run, profitable and increasingly well known.

The Ashworths seem to have been known to Bodmer from his time in Egerton; later letters between them suggest a mutual respect and friendship, speaking openly to each other and enquiring about their respective family members.

In 1825, the Ashworths had a water-wheel erected at New Eagley Mill, recruiting the engineering firm Fairbairn & Lillie to execute the works, along with other machine fittings. This working relationship between the Ashworths and William Fairbairn was an important factor in Egerton's development, because when, a couple of years later, Philip Novelli was struggling to find a buyer for his partially completed mill and dye works at Egerton, he approached Fairbairn requesting help in finding a buyer. Fairbairn later wrote:-

'I consulted with Mr. Lillie, and applied to a firm whose mills and property were situated a little further down the river. We were on intimate terms with the members of this firm, for whom we had erected a water-wheel, and done other work in their mills. They had very little spare capital, but they urged me to buy the estate, at a fixed price, and said they would join Mr. Lillie and me in converting the buildings into a cotton mill. The whole property was bought in our joint names for £13,000, each paying one-fourth of the purchase money.'

Any profit made by the new Egerton Mill was being invested back into the business, so little interest was returned to the proprietors in those early stages of operation. The four partners continued for a number of years, but the relationship between Fairbairn and Lillie became strained. This, coupled with the drain on Fairbairn and Lillie's capital caused by the investment in Egerton, prompted them to sell their shares in the mill and dye works to the Ashworths in 1832. Henry soon after became the senior partner and took particular responsibility for the Eagley mill, while Edmund took on management of Egerton Mill and the dye works, moving his family into the newly built Egerton Hall which overlooked the mill.

By 1835, the Egerton Mill was fully productive. Henry and Edmund Ashworth put into it the finest spinning machinery available. J. W. Cowell, one of the 1833 to 1834 Factory Commissioners, described Egerton Mill as one of the most efficient he had ever seen. He reported that '*The machinery in Mr. Ashworth's Egerton Mill is of the newest and most beautiful construction.*' The mill was described by visitors as clean looking and whitewashed, well ventilated and well lit with large windows.

The main showpiece of Egerton Mill was a waterwheel, powered by the waters of Eagley Brook, which was said to be one of the biggest in the United Kingdom. It was originally designed by Bodmer, but was left in an incomplete state when he left the country, its final construction being handled by Fairbairn & Lillie. Costing £4,800, it was 62 feet in diameter, revolved three times a minute, and delivered 110 to 140 horsepower. The large wheel was something of a novelty, and became a tourist attraction in the 1830s and 1840s, with a visitor's book being kept by it.

A later visitor to the mill described the activities there; the bales of cotton, imported from abroad through Liverpool, would arrive at the mill, be unpacked, sorted and thrown in the '*opener*' machine. This was the first process of cotton spinning, and the material then went through various stages, until it was at last converted into thread, and laid down on reels of all shapes and sizes in the packing room. The Ashworths were proud of their yarn, and regularly inspected it at the factory to ensure that it met their high standards of quality.

Henry Ashworth
of The Oaks
(1794 - 1880)

Edmund Ashworth
of Egerton Hall
(1800 - 1881)

Egerton Mill in 1883.

Three generations of Ashworth men in 1848

John Ashworth of Birtenshaw (1772 – 1855) far right, Edmund Ashworth Jun. of Egerton Hall (1833 – 1901) centre, Edmund Ashworth Sen. of Egerton Hall (1800 – 1881) left. (Reproduced with permission of Jason Wright).

Three generations of Ashworth women circa 1846/7

Isabel Ashworth née Thomasson (1771-1852) far right, Charlotte Ashworth née Christy (1805-1873) far left; Charlotte's only two daughters Rebecca Maria Ashworth (1838-1908) mid-left and Charlotte Anne Ashworth (1839-1870) mid-right. (Reproduced with permission of Jason Wright).

Edmund & Charlotte Ashworth with family, circa 1846
(Reproduced with permission of Jason Wright).

Edmund Ashworth Jnr. (1833-1901)   Rebecca Maria Ashworth (1838-1908)

The waterwheel at Egerton Mill was a
visitor attraction in the 1840s, and was
said to be one of the biggest in the
United Kingdom.

Egerton Hall, the home of Edmund Ashworth.
The hall stood where Woodland Grove now is.

Egerton Hall. The garden shown in this photograph
extended over what is now Brindle Dell, towards Blackburn Road.

Edmund Ashworth, jun., with his gamekeepers
outside Egerton Hall circa 1890.

Left to right:
James Berry, Henry Berry, Edmund Ashworth, Edmund Berry, James Berry jun.
Three brothers and the son of Henry.

Egerton Hall - Bolton Journal (1885).

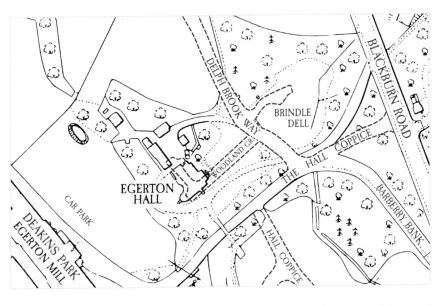

Map showing the location of Egerton Hall with modern road layout overlaid in red.

Advertisement for Ashworth's 'Egerton Silk Finish'
(The Wyndham Ashworth Family Archive).

A new product in 1879, Egerton Silk Finish was promoted as a replacement for silk: *'Largely used by Dress Makers, Mantle Makers and Hat Makers, for Quilting, and by workers in Leathers, who are accustomed to use the best qualities of silk.'*

Trade Marks (1880 Melbourne Exhibition Catalogue).

46

The Masters & Operatives

Visitors to the Ashworth mills were full of praise for the conditions of the workers, the Ashworth's concern for their employees and the orderliness with which the mill was run. Each operative was said to have fifty per cent more space than in most other mills; hot water, soap and towels were provided for all workers, and the overseers were charged with ensuring that all children washed thoroughly after breakfast. Work clothes were provided which were put on in segregated changing rooms for men and women.

One visitor to the mill, a reporter for a London newspaper, said that the Ashworths were in the *'constant and excellent habit of mingling familiarly and kindly with their workpeople, all of whom they are personally acquainted with'*.

The report also stated that *'...the women looked very obviously better than those in the town mills. Their faces, in hardly a single instance, wore that thoroughly blanched hue which is an almost unvarying characteristic of the city cotton spinners; while many of the girls had very perceptible roses in their cheeks. Their working dresses were scrupulously neat, and upon the shoulder of each was embroidered the name of its proprietor.'*

In return for the comfortable working environment, the workers had to conform to expected standards of conduct. All workers had to come to work clean and washed daily, changing their shirts twice a week. They started work at six o'clock and worked an eleven-hour day. Fines were imposed for lateness, being away from position, swearing or spoiled yarn. Anyone found to be under the influence of alcohol in work was fined 5 shillings. Seduction of mill operatives or their daughters was not tolerated: if the man did not marry the girl, he was dismissed. All workers were expected to attend church on Sundays.

The Ashworths' religious upbringing as part of the Society of Friends had instilled in them Quaker values; that each human being had a unique worth and was of equal value, and in the importance of community life. They also believed that the happiness, comfort and education of their workers, contributed to their own success. Like other Quaker family businesses of the Victorian era, they felt that treating people well was not only the right thing to do, but was also plain good business.

The Bolton Chronicle from Saturday 25th May 1850, recorded a social event arranged by the Ashworths, one of a number of examples of similar such entertainments they laid on:

'Messrs. H. & E. Ashworth gave a treat to the workpeople at new Eagley and Egerton mills, to the two British schools, and to other dissenting schools. A

47

procession was formed which visited each master's residence; after which the adults, about 700, sat down in decorated rooms to tea and sandwich, beef, ale, and porter being also introduced. The children, numbering about 500, were provided with coffee, currant bread, and buns. During the day 4 variegated balloons were sent up, one containing upwards of 100 sheets of double crown paper, made expressly for the occasion, by J. Lawson, news agent, of Bolton. The evening was spent by dancing and a display of fire-works.'

Another newspaper article from 1851 describes the half-yearly meeting of Egerton Reading Society, where 80 workmen and subscribers met at Egerton Mill's news and reading-room, for dinner. The mill owners had encouraged the establishment of this kind of literary society, creating an environment where their operatives could improve themselves, should they so desire. Henry once said in reference to the education of the workers, that he wished to *'enlarge their views, if possible, and to teach them not to be satisfied with the condition in which they were born.'*

A mill school was set up in 1831, initially as an infant school for the children of operatives. When the children reached the age of nine they would start working part time in the mill, and reduce their schooling hours to two hours a day. The literacy rates in Egerton and Eagley were considerably better than others in the industry, Henry claiming publicly in 1833 that 98 per cent could read and 45 per cent could write.

Given their genuine concern for the welfare of the working people, and their efforts to look after their workforce, it is perhaps understandable that the Ashworths resented government interference in the way they ran their business and treated their workers. They opposed the new factory legislation, which laid down rules restricting working hours, and employment of children.

The Ashworth brothers were also active in the Anti-Corn Law League. The Corn Laws kept bread prices artificially high by taxing imports. This was to the benefit of the landowners, but to the detriment of workers and factory owners (who had to increase wages as a result). Cobden Street and Bright Street in the centre of Egerton are named after the politicians Richard Cobden and John Bright, two of the Ashworth's fellow founder members of the League, whom they worked with for many years to promote the League's objectives.

When the mill had first been opened in the 1830s, workers were drawn from many neighbouring districts and from further afield. When labour was in short supply, the Ashworths promoted the creation of a labour migration scheme for out of work agricultural workers from the south. In total, they relocated eleven such families to Egerton, 54 people, who made up 6% of the workforce in 1836. An analysis of the 1851 census for central Egerton shows that 88 per cent of the population had been born in Lancashire, many from Turton itself, as well as Bolton, Edgworth, Darwen, Chorley, Wigan, Bradshaw, and many other towns and villages. The remaining 12 per cent were from other counties, including notably Yorkshire, Cheshire, Suffolk, Cumberland, Buckinghamshire, as well as some from Ireland.

Housing in Egerton

As they had done at Eagley, the Ashworths built substantial stone cottages for their workers to rent. The House of Lords Sessional Papers from 1833 recorded that the cottages at Egerton and Bank Top were superior to most in size, building and maintenance. In the following decade, Viscount Ebrington contrasted the terrible conditions of the London labouring class with those at Egerton, stating that:-

> '[the London workers] *pay in rent for their one miserable room as much as Mr. Ashworth of Egerton, a manufacturer such as this country may be well proud of, receives from his prosperous work people for cottages, which I saw containing five and six and seven rooms each, with every convenience.'*

Soon after the Ashworth brothers had taken on Egerton Mill, an outbreak of fever in the village prompted them to order periodic examinations of every cottage in their possession, to ensure the tenants were keeping them clean and that they were well ventilated and had appropriate bedding and furniture.

In 1832, Edmund Ashworth married Charlotte, the daughter of Thomas Christie of Broomfield in Essex. Thomas had been the proprietor of a hat manufacturing firm in London (Christie & Co. is still in business today), and had recently retired from the business, leaving it in the hands of family members. In the same year that his daughter married Edmund Ashworth, he purchased the Pinnacle field in Egerton, and financed the erection of thirty-three cottages on it.

The rating valuations for 1833 show that the Ashworths owned one quarter of the 200 or so properties in the area, including Bedford Row, Dewhursts, Smiths, Hamer Buildings, Egerton Hall and Egerton Old Hall. Six years on, another fifty cottages had been built, and through building and further acquisitions, the Ashworths had increased their share to a third of the overall quantity of property, including cottages on Egerton Vale, Stanrose, Egerton House, Bath Street and Old Globe.

The 1841 census shows that there were then about 290 properties in the Egerton area (including Dunscar and Dimple), housing some 1,600 inhabitants. By 1866, the Ashworths owned more than half of the houses in Egerton, having by then also acquired School Row, Kenyon Row and Old Swan.

In 1842, Edmund Ashworth was one of a number of contributors to a report requested by the Poor Law Commissioners into the sanitary conditions of the labouring population of England, which was presented at the Houses of Parliament. In it he described their cottages at Egerton, of which there were four basic types; his favoured model had three bedrooms, a living room (15 feet by 13 feet), a back kitchen (15 feet by 9 feet), with an oven, boiler and grate as fixtures, and a back yard. The roofs were covered with Welsh slates, and the timber used for carpentry and joinery was American pine, the whole cottage costing just over £103 to construct.

By the 1860s, the Ashworths had come to be the majority property owners in Egerton, but it is not true to say that they built the whole village, nor that they owned all of the houses. The existence of their mill had created a large part of the demand for housing, but many of the cottages on Blackburn Road, which give Egerton its character, were built by other local tradesmen and farmers. These included James Hamer, William Smith, James Horrocks, John Ratcliffe, Thomas Briggs, William Kenyon, James Barry, Thomas Armstrong and James Waters – each of whom had built blocks of cottages, usually three or four long, along the main road.

Cottages on Blackburn Road (Bolton News).
Smith Row in the foreground and Horrocks Row further up.

The shop sign is an advertisement for Will's Star Cigarettes.
The cottage was a grocery store in the mid-1900s, run by Jimmy Halton.

Ashworth's Plans of Egerton cottages from 1839.

Bedford Row.

The Dissolution of the Ashworth Partnership

In its early days, Egerton Mill had been well organised and ahead of the game in terms of mechanization. This technical edge only lasted a relatively short time though; there were hundreds of cotton spinning mills in Lancashire, more than fifty in Bolton alone, and the industry was highly competitive. The others caught up, and Egerton Mill soon became merely average.

In the late 1830s the profits at both Egerton and Eagley had declined, and the mills subsequently started to sustain some losses, although later returned to profitability.

This slide in operational superiority was exacerbated by the fact that both Edmund and Henry had started increasingly to leave the supervision of the mills to managers. They had now been partners in the firm for 30 years, and had a range of other interests which reduced their capacity to be able to personally supervise the businesses.

There was also an increasing animosity between the brothers, which led to disagreements, and a failure to cooperate. Henry's son Henry wrote in 1850 that '..*no good can ever be done until they separate...*'. Accordingly, in 1854, Henry and Edmund agreed to dissolve their partnership.

> *'THE PARTNERSHIP heretofore subsisting between the undersigned HENRY ASHWORTH and EDMUND ASHWORTH, in the business of Cotton-spinners and Manufacturers, carried on at the New Eagley Mills and also at the Egerton Mill, in the county of Lancaster, under the firm of "H. and E. ASHWORTH," EXPIRED this day by the effluxion of time.*
>
> *The business at the Egerton Mill will in future be carried on by the said EDMUND ASHWORTH and Others, under the firm of EDMUND ASHWORTH and SONS, and that at the New Eagley Mills will in future be carried on by the said HENRY ASHWORTH and Others, under the firm of HENRY ASHWORTH and SONS, by which latter firm all Debts due or owing to or by the late firm of H. and E. ASHWORTH will be received and paid. –*
>
> *Dated this thirtieth June, 1854.'*

The book value of Egerton Mill was at that point £62,575, and Edmund had 46% of the equity in it. He retired in 1864, leaving active control of the firm to his sons Edmund junior and Samuel.

Edmund died in 1881 aged 80, at the Prince of Wales Hotel, Southport, after being ill for two days. The report of his death in the Bolton Evening News gives us some insight into his involvement in local politics, and his public and business life. In 1860, he had served on nine public and three asylum committees. He was a County Magistrate, and first Chairman of Turton Local Board. He had at times served on the Board of Guardians for Little Bolton, Manchester Chamber of Commerce, Bolton New Waterworks Committee, and others.

The funeral was held on the morning of Friday 25 March at Christ Church Walmsley. The weather was bleak and wild, and the fields covered with snow. In the village, the window blinds were drawn as a mark of respect. According with the wishes of the deceased, the funeral was of a plain and simple character.

Family members gathered at Egerton Hall, from where the coffin, draped in black velvet, was borne by four gamekeepers, James, Edmund and Henry Berry and William Shorrocks, accompanied by Thomas Davies and Robert Mayoh (gardeners), James Mayoh (farmer), and James Haslam, William Richardson, Booth Waddicor, Thomas Howarth and John Haslam (old servants).

The procession was joined by about two hundred people at the front entrance to the Hall; retired servants, tenants, tradespeople and work people. They followed the path through the grounds of Egerton Hall, directly to the churchyard. The burial service was conducted by Rev. J. Stott, vicar of Walmsley.

The modest, now weathered gravestone can be seen at the church on the right hand side of the graveyard looking towards the church from Blackburn Road, enclosed by low iron railings along with the gravestones of other Ashworth family members. The archway in the wall by the side of it was the old entrance from the pathway through Egerton Hall's grounds.

Following Edmund Ashworth's death, many of the properties he owned in Egerton were sold. In July 1882, sales by auction were advertised in the local newspaper, which included the central shops, the Co-operative store, Dewhurst House, Dewhurst cottages, Old Globe cottages, Old Swan cottages, Hamers Houses, Egerton Vale and some cottages on the main road, as well as Stanrose Villa and Briggs Fold.

THE DEAKINS

The Egerton Dye Works Company

Deakin is another family name that is synonymous with Egerton. The Ashworth brothers had established the spinning mill and had been a key driving force in the development of the village from the 1830s, but it was the Deakins who picked up the baton and kept the mill going into the twentieth century, and made a number of significant contributions to village and community life.

The forerunner to the Deakins' bleaching and dyeing business had been set up when the mill was originally built. It was situated in the basement of the mill, and was kitted out by Bodmer with his *'self-acting machinery'*. The Ashworths operated the dye works, for a decade or so, but eventually decided to focus on spinning, and leased the dye-works out.

By the 1840s it had been taken on by four dyers, William Darbyshire taking the lead amongst them. While Darbyshire was in charge, a visitor from London inspected the works and made a description of it, part of which is reproduced here:-

> *'The dye-house at Turton consists of an immense apartment, which forms the basement story of a large cotton-mill. It is paved with stone, and supplied with a complete system of drainage for carrying off the spent dye stuffs and soiled water which result from each day's operations.*
>
> *On entering this apartment, the visitor is struck with what appears to be the confused assemblage of differently-shaped machines, unlike the sameness which is equally remarkable in the grouping of the machinery of a spinning or weaving-mill.*
>
> *Here are large stone cisterns for bleaching and for washing; dash-wheels, and other wheels, also for washing; vessels containing dye-stuffs, called dye-becks; others, containing soap and water, called soap-becks; mangles for rolling the cloth; others furnished with brushes for laying the fibres all in one direction; squeezing rollers for pressing the water from the goods; and a curious machine for drying goods by centrifugal force.'*

By the late 1840s, the business appears to have been having difficulties. In February 1847, Samuel Brewis, Nathan Newbould, John Smith and William Darbyshire, dissolved their partnership by mutual consent. The business was continued by Darbyshire and Smith, but lasted only two years before becoming bankrupt.

DYE-BECKS.

Sketches of Egerton Dye Works in the 1840s

WASHING BY STEAM-POWER.

Edward Carr Deakin (1824 – 1900) – Founder of Deakins

Around the time that Darbyshire and Smith were going out of business, a Congregational minister, Rev. James Deakin of Stand (near Whitefield), used to visit Egerton to preach occasionally. He would later retire from the ministry and move to Moss Cottages, next to Merry Cock Hall. He was described as a staunch Nonconformist, a cordial hater of modern innovations, and courageous in the defence of his opinions.

After preaching one day at Egerton, he got into discussion with John Haslam, a local quarry man, and happened to mention that his son, Edward, was 'marking time' as a clerk in the office of a Manchester cotton warehouse. Mr Haslam suggested the solution; the dye-works were now empty, and awaiting a new wave of industrial activity.

Edward Carr Deakin established himself there in the early 1850s, taking on only a small part of the works at first, and employing a few men. His right hand man was James Haslam, the son of his father's acquaintance who had suggested the venture in the first place. The Haslam family continued to be involved in the management of the dye works for a hundred years, over four generations.

He married Ann Grundy of Ringley in 1850, and over the following fifteen years the couple had four sons and three daughters; James, Henry Taylor, Edward, Louisa, Charles, Ada and Elizabeth. Their eldest son James married Alice, daughter of John Robinson, the Egerton village surgeon and doctor. James became a general practitioner and surgeon, and moved to Sale. The other three brothers, Henry, Edward Jnr. and Charles joined their father's business, although Charles soon left after a disagreement with his father.

A newspaper article from July 1869 tells of a church event hosted by Edward Carr Deakin, where the teachers, scholars, and congregation, 140 people in total, were invited to Cadshaw Brow for tea, games and ginger beer. After playing until they were weary, they walked in procession back to the residence of Mr Deakin – singing hymns and giving three cheers.

By 1871, 45 men and 8 boys were employed at Egerton Dye Works. In the following decade, as his sons became involved, the business expanded. The old, empty Belmont bleachworks was taken over and placed in charge of Edward Jnr. Later, Ryecroft Mill at Belmont was rebuilt and opened under Henry's management. The Deakins were credited with revitalising the village of Belmont. Many of the villagers had left when work ceased at the old mill, leaving empty cottages, and a population of only 100. Over the following few decades it was built back up to be a hardworking and prosperous village of about 750 people.

By 1881, Edward senior moved temporarily to Belmont, living firstly at Egremont House and then later Hill Top, before returning to Dewhurst House, Egerton, and leaving the two Belmont properties in the hands of his sons.

In 1892, Edward Carr Deakin purchased Egerton Dye Works from the executors of the late Edmund Ashworth for £20,000. A year later Deakins Ltd was registered with a share capital of £200,000 – the three directors being Edward Carr Deakin and his two sons Edward Deakin and Henry Taylor Deakin.

Edward Carr Deakin died on 3 April 1900, aged 76. His wife, Ann, his partner of fifty years, had died a few months earlier. He was said to have been deeply attached to her, and was never the same afterwards. His funeral was, as he requested, the plainest possible, with no coaches or flowers, attended only by representatives of the family. There was a short service, held at Dewhurst House, and the coffin was carried to the Egerton Congregational chapel yard by some of his workmen. The bleach works at Egerton and Belmont were closed for the day. The Celtic cross gravestone can still be seen at the front of the church.

His estate was valued at £203,942. In his will, he left £12,000 to his son Charles, and £10,000 each to James and Ada, his other children, the remaining estate being equally divided amongst his children. The bleaching business was continued under the management of his two sons Henry Taylor and Edward, who were already partners in the firm.

Left:
Entrance to the main office at Egerton Dye Works.

Above:
Dewhurst House, home of
Edward Carr Deakin and his
family, subsequently occupied
by Henry Taylor Deakin and
family.

Left:
Edward Carr Deakin
at Hill Top House, Belmont
in the 1890s

The lady is presumed to be
Ann, his wife.

Aerial view of Egerton Mill & Dye Works, Egerton Hall top right

Croft lads at Deakins Ltd in 1913.
William Hodgson seated on right.

Egerton Congregational (now United Reformed) Church in 1972 (Bolton News).

Edward Carr Deakin was described as being of a quiet and reserved disposition, an earnest Christian man with strongly grounded religious beliefs. In 1873, he contributed £300 to the cost of the rebuilding of the chapel, the total cost being £4,657.

Ladies at Egerton Congregational Sunday School in the mid-1880s.

2nd row up, 3rd from left Mary Ann Collier. Bottom row 1st from left Mary Dealey.

Henry Taylor Deakin (1853 – 1916) – Benefactor of Egerton Park

Henry Taylor Deakin was the second son of Edward Carr Deakin. He was born in Egerton in 1853, brought up at Dewhurst House, and educated at Rossall School. On 19 April 1883, he married Mary Grace Rawlins at Rugeley Congregational Church.

To commemorate the marriage, the firm gave a dinner at Ryecroft Works, for 300 employees and old people of the neighbourhood. The workers of Egerton Dye Works also held a celebration, a few days later, at the Cross Guns.

Their early married life was spent at Belmont, whilst the Ryecroft Mill there was under Henry's management. Their three children were born at Belmont; Henry 'Hal' in 1884, Margaret in 1890 (died in infancy), and Mabel Grace in 1892.

When his father died in 1900, Henry returned to Dewhurst House in Egerton.

Henry Taylor Deakin
(1853 - 1916)

Mary Grace Deakin
(1858 - 1944)

Egerton Playing Fields

On coming back to Egerton, Henry and his wife Mary wanted to improve amenities in the village and provide a safe area for children to play. In 1913, he purchased about four acres of land in the centre of the village from the Warburton Trustees. Plans, prepared by the architects Messrs. Bradshaw, Gass and Hope, were presented to Turton UDC, who approved them. After the work was completed, the park was transferred to the council for public use, forever.

The new playing fields included separate sets of swings for girls and boys, playing areas, a bowling green, and lawn tennis courts. The old farmhouse was made into a playing barn for children, and part became the caretaker's house. On the day the park opened, there were flags flying from buildings in the village, and Belmont Brass Band was in attendance.

Despite the rain, a large number of villagers came to watch the opening ceremony, where Mrs Deakin was presented with a ceremonial silver key by Mr Gass, who was representing the architects. Mrs Deakin was one of a number of people who spoke to the assembled crowd, saying that she felt a proud and happy woman at being able to open the playing fields, and closing with *'God bless this playing field!'*

Henry Deakin also spoke at the opening ceremony, saying that it was rather a relief for a moment to look at the bright side of things in such a period. He was referring to the outbreak of World War I, Britain having declared war four days earlier.

The war was still being fought two years later when, on the Christmas Eve of 1916, Henry died aged 63. He had caught pneumonia, having been suffering from a cold for the previous few weeks. He was buried at Egerton Congregational Church.

A eulogy published in the local newspaper said that he would be a much-missed man among the poorest people who always received his sympathetic attention. He had done a great amount of good in both Belmont and Egerton in an unassuming manner. He was described as a quiet, retiring, studious and thoughtful person.

The Deakins' generous gift has now been enjoyed by several generations of local families. In 2014, a well-attended gala was organised by local volunteers from the Egerton Park Improvement Committee, to celebrate the centenary of its opening.

Ceremonial Silver Key (Bolton Archives). The inscription reads:
'Egerton Playing Fields, opened by Mrs H. T. Deakin, August 8th 1914'.

Inscription commemorating Deakin's gift

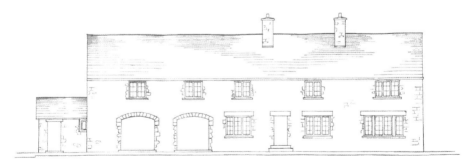

Egerton Park caretaker's cottage, shelter & store 1962 (Bolton Archives).

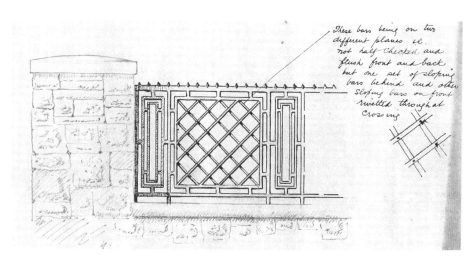

Design for wrought iron railings, Walter McFarlane & Co., Glasgow, c1913
(Bolton Archives).

Ladies outside the park shelter in the 1950s.
This structure has now been demolished, having become unsafe.

64

Children playing at Egerton Park in 1971 (Bolton News).

Aerial view of Egerton from the 1950s, Egerton park bottom right.

65

Edward Deakin and his Battles with Bolton Corporation

Henry's younger brother Edward had a different character than his father and brother. He was not, like them, quiet and reserved, but was assertive, even combative, and did not shy away from the public spotlight. He was described as an excellent host with fine appearance and courtly manners. He also was a vigorous defender of his business and his land rights.

He was born at Dewhurst House, and brought up in Egerton. When aged twelve he went to Rossall School, returning to Egerton at the age of eighteen to start working with his father. He married Eliza Isherwood in 1880 at Christ Church, Walmsley. They had four daughters named Jessie, Hilda, Ethel and Lucy, born at Ryecroft House, Belmont, and a son Edward Carr Deakin born at Hill Top.

Like his older brother, he based himself at Belmont when Deakins took over management of the works, but after his father died, vacated the mansion at Hill Top and moved to Egerton Hall, the old home of the Ashworths.

Edward's main recreational interest was shooting, and he held regular parties on Belmont and Darwen moors. When he was younger, he hunted with the Holcombe harriers, for a time being secretary of the hunt. A newspaper report from 1927 tells how members of the hunt, both mounted and on foot, gathered at Egerton Hall, and then followed the hounds down Longworth Valley in search of hares up towards Dimple and across the moors in the direction of Turton Tower.

Deakin was also a keen cricketer, becoming president of Egerton Cricket Club at the age of 23, and remaining in the position until his late sixties. The Deakin family contributed generously to the club over the years, making donations to building a club house, purchase of a mowing machine, drainage work and the erection of fencing.

In the first decade of the twentieth century, a series of legal disputes arose between Edward Deakin and Bolton Corporation. The Council wanted to ensure that the water supply was adequate for the town's growing population. Some of the planned works would take water from sources that were being used by Deakins Ltd, therefore potentially depriving the dye works of the water it needed. Additionally, some of the proposed reservoirs were on land owned by the Deakins, which was subject to compulsory purchase.

In 1904, Bolton Town Council petitioned Parliament for leave to bring a Bill to authorise construction of additional waterworks, and make other improvements to the town's utilities. The plan was opposed by a number of landowners and businesses, who complained that they would be disadvantaged by the scheme, including Deakins Ltd.

The House of Lords announced a settlement, giving the Deakins the protection they wanted; 1.7 million gallons of water per day would be released into Eagley Brook to allow their works to operate. They also seem to have negotiated an extension to their lease of the Belmont works.

Deakin had a stone monument erected in Belmont with an inscription describing exactly the concession that had been won for the protection of the dye works and the workers who were dependent on it. The monument still exists, on the corner of Maria Square.

Two years later, they were at loggerheads again. Bolton Corporation was using the powers granted to it by their Act of 1905 to purchase land for Delph Reservoir. The land to be occupied by the reservoir was partly on the Longworth estate, and partly on the Dimple estate – the latter being owned by Edward Deakin. Bolton Corporation Waterworks took 64 acres of land, including parts of Orrells Farm, Whittles Farm, New Farm and a small part of Howarths Farm.

The Corporation valuers said the land was worth between £3,000 and £4,000, regarding it as agricultural land. Deakin argued that the site had natural characteristics such as its elevation and water supply, which made it ideal as a reservoir site, and therefore it was worth more than mere agricultural land. In fact, they themselves had contemplated building a reservoir there for the use of their business. Deakin valued the land at £19,700. They settled at £8,197.

Eight years later Deakin was again in conflict with Bolton Corporation, this time about the road along the embankment of the reservoir at Belmont, the Corporation claiming it was private land, Deakin claiming it was public. He had instructed the locals to break down the gates and force the locks. On horseback, he headed a procession that marched over the road, cheered on by a band, and delivered an address in which he urged the people to assert their rights. Bolton Corporation took Deakin to court to get an injunction against him, and to claim damages for trespass.

Edward Deakin (1854 - 1935)   Eliza Deakin (1857 - 1931)

The Royal Lancashire Agricultural Show, 20th July 1920 at Lostock
Edward Deakin attending in capacity of High Sherriff.
Top row *(7) Edward Deakin - 7th from left,* ***Bottom row:*** *(3) Mrs. Deakin,*
(4) Lord Leverhulme and (5) Duke of York (later King George VI).

68

Bolton Corporation Bill.

THE BATTLE WITH THE DISTRICTS.

URBAN COUNCILS' DEMANDS.

TERMS ARRANGED WITH DEAKINS.

Headlines in the Bolton Evening News confirming agreement reached
with Edward Deakin regarding acquisition of land for Delph Reservoir in 1905.

Members of the Waterworks Committee of Bolton Corporation
present at the cutting of the first sods on the site of Delph Reservoir,
4 June 1908. (Bolton Archives ABZ/66/99).

69

Egerton Lads Club & Swimming Baths

Coinciding with older brother Henry's gift of Egerton playing fields to the local people, Edward decided to make his own contribution, in the form of a new building for the Lads Club.

Around 1894, Egerton Lads Club had been established, and in the first decade of the nineteen hundreds, they were using the old church hall on Water Street, then known as the Oddfellows and Foresters Hall. In 1912, Edward Deakin, who was president of the Lads Club, purchased the old church hall from the Egerton Foresters, and had it pulled down to make way for a new clubhouse and swimming baths. The architects were Ormerod and Pomeroy, and the cost about £2,000.

The new swimming bath was opened in 1914. It was covered over when the room was needed for other purposes, such as gymnastic classes that were held in winter. It was not a public swimming baths; the Lads Club Committee only allowed the pool to be used by residents of Egerton and Belmont, and anyone living beyond the finger post at the junction of Darwen Road and Blackburn Road was debarred.

Mrs. E. Deakin with boys and girls sports teams, at Egerton Hall (1920s).

High Sheriff of Lancashire

In 1920, Edward Deakin was appointed as High Sheriff of Lancashire, a ceremonial role lasting for one year, given as a mark of respect and bestowed by the King.

The papers relating to Deakin's shrievalty are at Bolton Archives, and include, letters offering congratulations on his appointment, invitations, acceptances and refusals for various events, public engagements, dinners, luncheons, dances, and correspondence with High Sheriffs from other counties.

The Shire Hall at Lancaster Castle houses a display of almost 600 shields bearing the arms of every High Sheriff of Lancashire since 1160, including one for Edward Deakin.

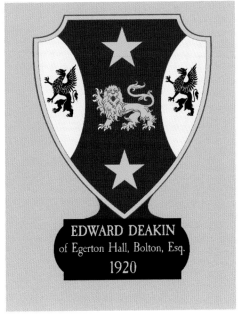

EDWARD DEAKIN
of Egerton Hall, Bolton, Esq.
1920

Edward Deakin in regalia as High Sheriff of Lancashire.

An illustration of Edward Deakin's shield at Shire Hall, Lancaster Castle.

The Compulsory Purchase of the Dimple Estate

In 1898, the Deakin family had purchased the Dimple estate from Peter Arthur Marsham Hoare, with a further acquisition the following year from Thomas Stevens and John Barnes. The purchase was made, Edward later said, so that water supply to Egerton Works could be preserved.

In 1922, Bolton Corporation was empowered to acquire large parts of the estate, 705 acres in total. They wanted to pull down the small farms and cottages, which they feared might contaminate the water.

The farms affected by the proposal were to the north of Egerton stretching up to Turton Moor; Coopers, Rushtons, Gregsons, Moss Side, Kenyons, Stones Bank, New & Top o'th' Meadow, Parrs, Orrells, Whittles, and parts of Horridges and Buffs, three cottages at Merry Cock Hall, fifteen cottages at Dimple with allotments, as well as 189 acres of moorland.

One of the surveyors said that all the houses were old and well worn, and that much of the land was rough in character, part swamp, and not of any first class agricultural bearing.

The Corporation attempted to ascertain a suitable compensation value for Deakin, but he was uncooperative. He claimed the value of the property was £200,000, but refused to give any details. They subsequently served him with notice, and he responded saying he would not put his hand to signing away a single acre of the Dimple property. He refused to make a claim, or furnish particulars.

He would neither agree, nor disagree, with their valuations. In interviews and meetings, the attitude he adopted, they said, *'precluded any possibility of coming to an agreement'*. The Corporation therefore used their compulsory powers.

When the dispute was referred to arbitration, Deakin firstly objected about the person appointed to arbitrate, and when that individual was replaced, refused to attend the meetings, or negotiate. Bolton Corporation applied to the Commissioners for Inland Revenue for a valuation of the property, and the arbitrator fixed a price of £15,414 following their report.

Deakin made no steps to convey the land to the Corporation, so they brought an action in the Chancery Court. In 1927, he was eventually forced to sign the conveyance. Resisting to the last, he marked the document as *'Signed under Parliamentary force majeure'*.

During the dispute, hundreds of letters passed between Deakin, his solicitors, and Bolton Corporation, in a process that had taken five years. One Corporation official showed his frustration when he complained that everything possible had been done to accommodate Mr. Deakin, but that he had behaved with *'childish petulance'*. Others closer to Deakin were more sympathetic, seeing his intransigence as a heroic resistance against the tyranny of the local authority. Alexander Le Marchant, the minister of Mawdsley Street, and a friend of Deakin, said that he was *'currently battling in vain to maintain his rural exclusivity against the incursions of Bolton Corporation'*.

Some of the farmsteads affected by the ownership transfer had been tenanted by local families for hundreds of years. The demolition of the old buildings meant that the tenants had to go elsewhere, and the labour employed had to find alternative work, or leave the district. The scattered ruins of some of the farms can still be seen.

Edward Deakin attending court with barristers.

73

Deakin's guests at a shoot at Lords Hall, Darwen Moor.

Back: Dr Smith, Mr. B. Garnett, Mrs. & Mr E. Hick Ashworth. Front: Mr E. Deakin, Mr. C.
Garnett, Mrs. Gordon Shorrock, Mr. Gordon Shorrock, Mrs. E. Deakin.

Edward Deakin with staff at Lords Hall, Darwen Moor.

Back: Deakin's butler, Bill Bolton, Bill Forest, Albert Croft, Deakin's gardener, ?, ?, Bob Croft,
Jim Bentley, G. Hodgson, Bill Ingham (Darwen gamekeeper), Edward Deakin.
Front: Bill Booth, Dick Isherwood, Horace Jenkins, ?, ?, ?. Bob Croft, Billy Robinson.

74

The Final Decades of Deakins Ltd

After the death of Edward Deakin in 1935, his son Edward Carr Deakin (1892-1942) of Dimple Hall (grandson of the original Edward Carr Deakin), became Chairman and Managing Director of the company. The Belmont works were making a loss, and insufficient profit was being made by Deakins Ltd overall to pay dividends. The firm's accountant urged Deakin to economise, curtailing family funding for Belmont Congregational Church and the social institutions at Egerton and Belmont, and cutting out any *'dead wood'* from the business.

In May 1936, he wrote to Deakin, saying that *'the various institutions will have to work out their own salvation and endeavour to obtain financial assistance from other quarters. It seems rather a callous attitude on my part but I do assure you that I fully appreciate your sentimental obligations. At the same time I think that you must take a firm stance otherwise you will have a very thin time.'*

Deakins Ltd were by no means alone in facing lean times during this period; the 'Great Slump' of the 1930s was the worst economic downturn of the 20th century. The decline was felt right across the Lancashire textiles industry. Cotton manufacturing in Britain had peaked in 1912, and World War I had caused foreign markets to close up. Other countries started to produce their own cloth, and by 1933 Japan had become the world's largest cotton manufacturer. In between the two wars, 345,000 workers left the industry and 800 mills closed. The first two generations of Deakins had been fortunate to be at the head of the business in more prosperous times.

In 1942, all production was moved to Egerton Mill. The Belmont Bleach & Dye Works were taken over by the Smith brothers, the sons of Dr Smith, whose wife was one of the Deakin family. Edward Carr Deakin died in that year, and his cousin, Henry 'Hal' Deakin, eldest son of Henry T. Deakin, became the head of the company.

In 1963, a notice was placed on the bulletin board at Deakins Ltd, Egerton Dye Works, which announced that the firm would be closing under a Government scheme for reorganising the textile finishing industry. The scheme promised to give the industry some new life, and the workpeople (numbering 160 at the time) compensation. It was thought to be better than hanging on for a few more years battling against impossible conditions.

The Mill Buildings

In 1898, E. Ashworth & Sons Ltd was one of fourteen firms combined to form the English Sewing Cotton Company. It was sold for £65,000, and it was later said that it had been well known that Egerton Mill was not in pristine condition. In 1906, J. & P. Coats Ltd of Paisley, having already previously acquired Eagley Mill, also acquired Egerton Mill. Only the buildings and land were sold, the business carried on in the mills was transferred to other establishments worked by the English Sewing Cotton Company.

In 1909, it was announced that the mills would shortly be closing due to their dilapidated state, but four years later the buildings were acquired by the Deakin family. Deakins Ltd closed in 1963, and the final textile business at the mill shut its doors in 1971. By the 1980s the mill buildings, known then as Deakins Industrial Estate, had multiple industrial uses, and were part derelict.

In the mid-1990s the site was acquired by Charles Topham & Sons Ltd and in 1998, despite some objections from local residents, they started to convert the buildings into offices. From 2002, Deakins Park became mixed use as office and residential accommodation.

Egerton Mills

Egerton Mill in the 1980s, then Deakins Industrial Estate,
at the time partly derelict.

Deakins Park in 2005.

CHAPTER 8   THE HOUSING ESTATES

Following the death of Edward Deakin in 1935, Egerton Hall was vacant until 1940, when it was occupied by North London Homes for the Blind for thirteen years. After that, it was again left empty. It was demolished in 1956. Deakins Ltd sold the Egerton Hall estate in 1961 to a property developer named Bob Horrocks.

Lancashire County Council had predicted that an additional 10,000 people would be living in Turton by 1983, and that 5,470 dwellings would be needed. A report in the Bolton Journal in 1965, under the headline *'The drift from Bolton goes on relentlessly – Many went to Turton'*, described how in the previous ten years, 6,000 people had left Bolton, and that Turton's population had increased by a similar amount.

In anticipation of further population increases, Turton UDC drew up a plan to preserve and improve amenities, at the same time as providing for extra homes, schools and shops. The plan was designed to protect the district from uncontrolled, unplanned, suburban sprawl.

The new residents would be concentrated in three main areas, Egerton forming part of *'Residential Area No. 2'* with Bromley Cross. Lancashire County Council approved the plans on the 3 February 1966. At that point, consent had already been granted for the residential development of 188 acres of land, to meet housing demands for the next 10 years.

In 1965, a new residential estate was already under way on the Egerton Hall and Dewhurst Farm estates, including Dewhurst Clough Road, Delph Brook Way, East & West Walk, Briarfield, Millgate and Woodland Grove. More homes were being built at Shorefield Mount, which had been under development since the early 1960s.

In 1966, Land Development & Building Ltd, another of Bob Horrocks's companies, submitted plans for 77 dwellings between Cox Green Road and Blackburn Road, as well as making amendments to their already approved plans for 25 houses and 41 bungalows at The Hall Coppice.

By 1970, the construction of the housing estates was complete or well under way. There would be 450 dwelling houses on the Stanrose & Cox Scar estates, 83 on The Hall Coppice estate, 145 or so on the Egerton Hall Estate, 90 on the Higher Dunscar Estate, 80 on the Shorefield Mount estate, with 120 in the Fairfield/Smith Lane area.

Egerton Hall during demolition in 1956 (Bolton News).

Letterhead of James Horrocks Estates from 1970.

In 1971, Egerton's only primary school, Walmsley C of E, refused to accept any more pupils, because of gross overcrowding. It was designed for only 200, and would soon have nearly 300. The building of the planned Egerton County Primary School had been delayed due to difficulties over land purchase. After a 13 month delay, the 3.8 acres of land behind the Cross Guns was acquired for £34,467, and building work was able to commence. The school opened in 1972.

In 1976, Milbury Homes advertised luxury split level bungalows at Higher Dunscar. Six years later, Bellway housing advertised four bedroom detached houses on Dimple Park.

From the start, there were anxieties among the local residents about the housing developments. Some later said that the place had been altered out of all recognition. It was no longer a village with a separate identity, they said, but more a suburb of Bolton.

Bob Horrocks, a property developer and one time Conservative councillor, was one of the principal actors in the creation of the early Egerton housing estates. For many years, he lived in the village at Thirlston, near to the war memorial. Born in 1923, he was the son of James Horrocks of Bolton, a house erector and building contractor.

Bob Horrocks built Metroland and Brytac, the holding companies for his property operations, into a multi-million pound business, undertaking many development projects in and around Bolton and further afield. In 1993, he featured in the Sunday Times 'secret rich list', with a personal fortune reportedly said to be £24m.

Street Names

Echoes of the past can be seen in some of the road names chosen on the new estates. Horridge Fold, Whittle Hill, Torra Barn Close and Goose Cote Hill are all named after old farms on the moors overlooking Egerton and Turton.

Shorefield can be found on an account from 1746, which recorded the acreage and tithe payments due by the residents of Turton. It was one of many fields held by John Horrocks of Dunscar, measuring one acre and two perches, out of his total area of forty-four acres at Dunscar and Dimple.

Hall Coppice refers to Egerton Hall, being only forty or so metres away from where the Hall stood.

Thomas Briggs who was the farmer at Stanrose from the 1830s, gave his name to Briggs Fold, and subsequently to Briggs Fold Road and New Briggs Fold.

Little Stones Road and Great Stone Close remember the Stones estate. Stones cottages, now demolished, were situated just above what is now the Higher Dunscar housing estate. They were part of the Stones estate that was the property of the Horrocks family in the eighteenth century. It is not difficult to guess the inspiration for the property name, given its proximity to the old quarries.

Pinnacle Drive was built on, or near to, Pinnacle Field; the same field that Thomas Christie had taken part of, to build Bedford Row in 1833.

Dewhurst Clough was built on land that originally formed part of the Dewhurst estate. Evan Dewhurst, yeoman of Turton was recorded in the Protestation Returns of 1642, and died in 1664. Part of the estate stayed in the possession of the Dewhursts until the early nineteenth century, being referred to in the will of John Dewhurst who died in 1817.

Druids Close is a nod to the Bronze Age stone circle on Chetham Close. The stones in the *'druidical circle'*, as described in the early nineteenth century, were apparently sledgehammered by a local farmer in the 1870s, said to be irritated by visitors to the site walking across his land. The remains of the ruined circle are still there, although there is little to see, with vegetation increasingly covering what is left.

Thankfully though, much of Egerton's heritage survives. The area has retained the character of a 19th century rural mill village, pleasantly set against its moorland backdrop.

More than half of the buildings shown on the 1795 map still exist today, including the seventeenth century Howarth Fold, Dunscar Fold and the older part of Dimple Hall. The majority of the stone cottages built along Blackburn Road in the early 1800s still stand strong, some now over two centuries old. Some of the factory buildings that formed the original Egerton Mill are still there, refurbished and put to new purpose. Many of the church buildings and public houses that served the community in the 19th century, still do so in the early 21st century.

Dunscar Fold

Listed as a Grade II building in 1967.

Inscription over shippon door is dated 1706.

H
I M

Dimple Hall in 1972. A date stone above the side entrance has the date 1688 and initials GIG. The southwest wing was added in 1835.

It was previously known as Sergeant Welchs, Thomason's and as Dimple Hall from the 1880s.

Howarth Fold Farm, photographed in 1989. Previously known as Isherwoods, the Howarth family occupied the farm in the 1700s.

Listed as a Grade II building in 1986.

82

Dunscar House

Built in the 1830s, it became a Grade II listed building in 1976.

The Dunscar Conservation Area report describes it as *'a gentleman's residence set in its own grounds, overlooking Eagley Valley.'*

Higher Dunscar House

Built in the 1880s for Ernest Greg.

In 1780, 12 acres of land plus buildings at Higher Dunscar were put up for sale *'late the Inheritance of Thomas Horrocks, a Bankrupt.'*

Two ladies on Blackburn Road, at the entrance to Higher Dunscar in the early 1900s.

The old cobbled road and walls can still be seen today.

Egerton House in the 1980s

Built in the 1830s, it was originally occupied by a businessman called Thomas Appleton.

In the early 1900s it was occupied by Edmund Hick Ashworth, who married Hilda Deakin.

The Egerton House Gatehouse

In 1971, Desmond and Birte Deakin converted Egerton House itself into a hotel and restaurant.

It continued operating as a hotel until 2014.

Egerton Barn datestone
A 1835

The barn was originally part of Egerton Farm, but was later transferred to Egerton House.

The Egerton
Co-operative Society
store was originally
part of Dewhurst
House until 1889.

It moved to the new
premises because the
old ones were too
small.

Another view of
the old Co-
operative shop at
Dewhurst House
taken prior to
1889.

Officials at the Egerton Co-
operative (c1890).

Back: Nicholas Fish, Joe Talbot,
John Holden.

Front: ?, William Edward
Chadderton, ?

Plans for the new Co-operative building were approved by the local board in 1889.

Co-operative Society cake box on display in Bakers Tea Room *'The Three Es'* (Egerton, Eagley and Edgworth), Bakery Department.

In the late twentieth century the left hand side of the premises was a hardware store named *Handyland*, until the proprietor Charlie James retired.

It is now Bakers Tea Room. The other part is the Skylark chip shop.

(Bolton News)

In July 1913, King
George V passed
through Egerton on
his way back from
laying the
foundation stone
for the King
George's Hall in
Blackburn.

Egerton
Conservative Club
building which stood
where the Thomas
Egerton pub car park
is now.

The building in the
centre of the picture
is now Crabtree's
shop. It was built on
'Little Field' part of
which had been
leased from George
Warburton in 1828.

Bedford Street
precinct under
construction in
1973.

The cottages on
the left have a date
stone *'Vesper
Terrace 1877'.*

(Bolton News)

Right:

Cottages on
Blackburn Road in
central Egerton.

Below:

Egerton Vale.

88

King William IV

The licensee in the 1830s was John Horrocks.

The pub has also been known as the Thomas Dutton, Baraccos, and is now Ciao Baby, an Italian restaurant.

(Bolton News)

The Cross Guns

The original Cross Guns was on Cox Green Road next to Walmsley Old Chapel. Roger Bromily was the licensee between 1744 and 1764, followed by John Horrocks from 1765 to 1780.

Mason's Arms

Taken from the access road to Egerton Mill (now Barberry Bank). The sign above the pub says *'Nuttall's Ales & Stouts'*.

Egerton Arms

The licensee was Ann Spencer from 1871 to 1891. Closed as a public house in 1912.

This building was the village post office in the late 1900s.

The Church Inn

Helme Horrocks was the licensee in the 1870s. Mrs Dunkerley and Mary Alice Wheeled[?] pictured above c1920. 120/122 Blackburn Road.

One Horse Shoe

Amos Crook leased land to his brother in law, George Warburton, who built this cottage. Harry Howarth (pictured above) was the licensee in 1902. 307 Blackburn Road.

Looking up Longworth Road towards Blackburn Road.

Date stone on cottages attached to The Globe.

Robert & Alice Edge.

Robert Edge was the landlord of The Globe from 1829. He died in 1853.

Blackburn Road looking northwards from the entrance to Egerton Park.

Apart from the cobbles and lack of cars, it looks exactly the same now.

(Bolton News)

Looking up Blackburn Road from outside The Globe, with the Conservative Club in the foreground.

Opened in 1901 by Lord Stanley, M.P., Financial Secretary to the War Office.

It was later used as a social club and contained a small library.

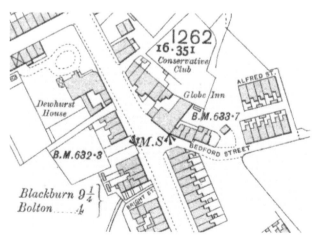

1910 25" OS map, showing The Globe Inn and Conservative Club.

The club house was demolished in 1963.

Christ Church Walmsley

Originally completed in 1839, the building was designed by Lancaster architect Edmund Sharpe.

The entrance to Christ Church Walmsley.

The Ashworth family gravestones are twenty metres or so up the pathway on the right hand side.

1902 Edward VII Coronation Celebrations at Walmsley.

Upwards of 400 old folk were entertained and had tea at the schoolroom at Walmsley, each of them being given a Coronation cup & saucer.

(Bolton Archives)

Walmsley National School was built in 1839. Adam Lomax Howarth granted the plot of land at Higher Dunscar to Rev. Slade, the Vicar of Bolton, and others.

(Bolton News)

Walmsley School Class in 1921

Headmaster
Mr. Bramwell
Row 1: ?, Ellen Isherwood, ?, ?, Edith Catterall, ?
Row 2: ?, ?, ?, ?, ?, ?, Jack Haworth, ?
Row 3: ?, ?, ?, ?, Margaret Catterall, Annie North, Hilda Green[?], ?, ?
Row 4: ?, ?, ?, Andrew Horrocks, ?, ?

Stanrose Terrace on Blackburn Road, curving round onto Mason Street.

Egerton Congregational
Church in 1887

The plot of land was
bought from John Nuttall
in 1812 *'Dewhurst's
Great Meadow'*.

Egerton Methodist Church

Built in 1891, it closed as a
chapel in 1963.

Now known as Vale
House, it was used as a
builder's ironmongery
warehouse in the 1970s
and 80s and is now mixed
use retail & residential.

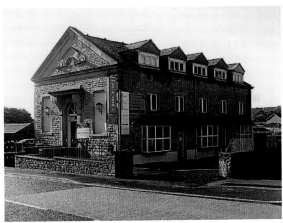

Walmsley Unitarian
chapel, also known as
Probert's Chapel.

Built 1713 on land
called *'The Dimples'*,
leased from
Christopher Horrocks
on a peppercorn rent.

Dunscar War Memorial erected in 1921.
Bears the names of 132 servicemen who died during the First World War.

Cox Green Farm in foreground, and The Rock Inn right of centre.

Victoria Farm, Dimple in 1965.

Labelled as *'Old Andrews'* and *'Morris' tenement'* on old maps. Operated as a beer house called The Queen Victoria in the 1800s.

Dimple Row prior to demolition in the 1960s.

Labelled as *'Peeping Row'* on the 1850 Ordnance Survey map shown below.

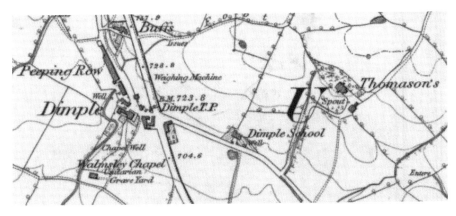

BIBLIOGRAPHY AND REFERENCES

- The Ashworth Cotton Enterprise, Rhodes Boyson, 1970.
- Bury Grammar School: A History, Ian B. Fallows, 2001.
- Records of the Manor Court of Turton, Sir James Lees Knowles, 1900.
- Who Lived in a House Like This? (Book II), Jean M. Boardman, 2017.
- Deakins Centenary Booklet, Deakins Ltd, 1950.
- A History of the Parish of Flixton, D.H. Langton, 1991.
- Humphrey Chetham, S. J. Guscott, 2003.
- Notes relating to the District of Turton, James C. Scholes, 1882.
- Various volumes: The Record Society of Lancashire & Cheshire, Lancashire Parish Register Society, The Chetham Society.

Archive Material

Bolton Archives

- Parish registers.
- Maps (ZAL1342 & ZAL1292).
- Deakin papers (ZDEH).
- Robert Walch papers (ZWL).
- 1833 Turton valuation (PTU3/4).
- Turton accounts (PTU1/2).
- Bolton Corp. vs Deakin (ABCS).

National Archives

- Crosse v Kay C/11/1719/22.
- Crosse v Latus C11/1503/16.
- Crosse v Critchley 11/1849/6.

John Rylands Library, Manchester

- Clowes deeds (CLD).

TLHS Archives

- Helen Heyes papers.
- Robert Walch papers.

Lancashire Archives

- Turton deeds (DDX1423).
- Wills (WCW).
- Quarter Sessions (QSP).
- Nuttall letters (DDX210).
- Hulton family (DDHU).
- Ashworth papers (DDAS).
- Holworthy papers (DDX291).
- Land Tax (QDL).

In addition, various newspaper articles from the Bolton Journal, Bolton Evening News, and others. A more detailed list of references can be found on the following web page: http://www.turtonhistory.com/2019/07/egerton.html.

APPENDIX A
List of Early References to the Walmsley Family in Turton

Chronological list of miscellaneous references to the Walmsley family of Turton between 1407 and 1648.

1407 - Marriage license granted by the Archdeacon of Chester to Alice de Walmsley, and Richard, son of William Thomasson of Turton. In the same year a quitclaim was dated at Bolton, from Alice de Walmsley, to Richard son of William Tomlinson [sic] of Turton. *(L.A. DDX1423/5536/18).*

1493 - In his will, Sir James Harrington of Wolfage Manor, Brixworth, bequeathed a messuage in Turton, in the holding of James *Walmesley*, to Myles Worsley. *(T.N.A. PROB 11/11/338).* Note that in 1520, the inquest at the death of Isabella, widow of Sir James Harrington recorded that she held property in various places including Turton, Longworth and Blackrod. *(p128, Lancashire Chantries, Chet. Soc., Vol 59).*

1562 - A suit was instituted by John Orrell, Esq., lord of the manor of Turton, complaining that Christopher Horrocks and 20 others, including James Walmsley, destroyed his new enclosure on Turton Moor. Thirteen out of the twenty men are named: Christopher Horrocks, John Horrocks, Alexander Longworth, Anthony Green, Ralph Green, George Horwich, James *Walmesley*, Ralph Brownlow, John Brownlow, Edward Warde, John Rothwell, Richard Wood, and Lawrence Wood. *(History of the House of Orrell, Terence Orrell, 1990, pp165-166).*

1566 - Agreement signed at Bolton between John Orrell and James Walmsley, Ralph Greene of Turton, Lawrence Brownlow and Lawrence Bradshaw of Tonge. The 1566 document, probably relating to Turton Moor, has not been located, but is referred to in the 1577 indenture. *(L.A. DDX1423/5536/14).*

1576 - Lawrence Brownlow son and heir apparent of Roger Brownlow of Tonge, gent, Ralph Green, son and heir apparent of Anthony Green of Turton, Lawrence Bradshaw of Tonge and James Walmsley of Turton agreed to combine their *'antient dedes evidence and wrytinge'* relating to commons and pastures in Turton, together in a chest, for which would be made a lock and four keys. *(L.A. DDX1423/5536/11).*

1577 - At the house of Oliver Pilkington in Charnock, an agreement was made between Walmsley, Green, Brownlow, Bradshaw, plus John Horrocks and Richard Worthington of Blainscough, to combine together to share litigation costs of any suits with Orrell. *(L.A. DDX1423/5536/14).*

1581 - James Walmsley of Turton, yeoman, enfeoffed lands in Turton *'lately enclosed from the moor and half of Walmsley Chapel yard'* to trustees for the use of his wife Agnes, and sons; William, John, Christopher, Roger, George, Charles and James. *(L.A. DDX1423/5536/1)*.

1581 - William Orrell, lord of the manor of Turton, attempted to come to an agreement with Lawrence Brownlow, Richard Worthington, Richard Wood, John Wood, John Horrocks, Ralph Green, Lawrence Bradshaw and James Walmsley, to release their rights to land on Turton Moor. This agreement may never have been finalised; it is signed by Lawrence Brownlow only. *(L.A. DDX1423/5536/10)*.

1582 - William Walmsley, eldest son and heir of James Walmsley, late of Turton, granted two parcels of land in Turton to Ralph Green, in exchange for land lately enclosed from Turton Moor called *Stanroos* (Stanrose). *(L.A. DDX1423/5536/22)*.

1593 - William Walmsley was recorded as a debtor to William Bromiley of Longworth, for twelve ewe sheep, and James Walmsley's widow for ten sheep. *(L.A. WCW)*.

1597 - An inventory of the estate of Edward Hopkinson of Edgworth records James Walmsley as his largest debtor for the sum of £8 6s. *(L.A. WCW/Sup/C24/48)*.

1598 - The widows of James Walmsley and William Walmsley contribute to the poor rate for Turton and Longworth. *(L.A. DDX1423/5536/14)*.

1602 - Christopher Walmsley was paid 2 shillings for providing two days labour to the building of a new mill at Turton. *(L.A. DDX1423/5536/14)*.

1608 - Will and inventory of Agnes Walmsley of Turton, widow of James Walmsley. Makes provisions for her sons John, Christopher, George, Charles, James, Andrew, daughter Elizabeth, and eldest son's wife Ellen. Also gives 10 shillings to the *'repayinge of Walmisley Chappell'*. *(L.A. WCW/Inf/C1326A/55)*.

1614 - James Walmsley, Christopher Horrocks, Lawrence Brownlow and James Roscoe compiled an inventory of the goods of William Mather of Turton. *(L.A. WCW/Supra/C59C/9)*.

1615 - James Walmsley appointed as one of the executors of the will of Richard Kay of Elton, his father-in-law. *(L.A. WCW)*.

1615 - Will of Anthony Green of Turton, gentleman. Bequeathed £20 to Christopher Horrocks and James Walmsley of Turton to be employed at their discretion to the best advantage of the maintenance of a preacher at Walmsley Chapel. *(L.A. WCW/Supra/C61B/22)*.

1619 - James Walmsley of Turton gave evidence under oath as a juror at a number of inquisitions post mortem at Bolton-le-Moors. *(Rec. Soc. Lanc. & Ches, Vol. XVI, 1887).*

1623 – Will of Katherine Kaye of Widdel, widow, late wife of Richard Kaye. James Walmsley, her son-in-law, was appointed as executor, husband of her daughter Katherine. James Walmsley was also listed as a debtor for £11 11s 0d. *(L.A. WCW/Supra/C85C/3).*

1623 - James Walmsley, Christopher Horrocks and Edward Hopkinson acted as trustees for Richard Orrell, in relation to his estate of 175 acres of land in Edgworth. *(Rec. Soc. Lancs. & Ches., Vol. XVII, 1888, p418-419).*

1627 - Lease for two hundred and ninety nine years by William Orrell of Turton, esq., to Humphrey Chetham of Clayton, gentleman, James *Walmisley* of Turton, gentleman, and Francis Isherwood of the same, gentleman, of Turton Tower with appurtenances and of messuages, etc. in Turton, Wigan and Edgworth. *(J.R.L. CLD/1175).*

1628 - Lease for one hundred years by Humphrey Chetham of Clayton, esq., Radcliffe Assheton of Cuerdall, esq., Richard Bannester of Breightmet, gentleman, Humphrey Booth of Salford, gentleman, and John Dawson and John Gillam, both of Manchester, gentlemen, to James *Walmisley* of Turton, gentleman, of a messuage in Turton. *(J.R.L. CLD/1179).*

1628 - Bond of Humphrey Chetham to James *Walmesley* of Turton, gentleman, for a lease to the latter of premises and land in Turton for one hundred years. *(J.R.L. CLD/1178).*

1630 – Depositions at the Court of the Duchy of Lancaster. Richard Orrell v. William Orrell, Humphrey Chetham, Francis Isherwood, James Walmsley. *(T.N.A. DL4/80/20).*

1633 - James Walmsley witness to the signing of the will of Roger Walkden of Sharples, who left £10 for the augmentation of Walmsley Chapel. *(L.A. WCW/Supra/C110C/21).*

1633 – James *Walmisley* was paid 3 shillings for providing one days labour loading timber *'out of the woods to the Tower'* for the building of a kiln at Turton. *(L.A. DDX1423/5536/32).*

1634 - James Walmsley was sent by Humphrey Chetham to Lancaster Castle, to negotiate his contribution to the cost of provisions and housekeeping at the Lancaster assizes. *(p144, The Foundations in Manchester, Hibbert / Ware).*

1637 - Indenture relating to 20 acres of land in Turton, leased in 1637 by George *Walmysley*, for the lives of himself, his wife Elizabeth and eldest son John, also making provisions for his other sons George and William. Date of indenture is worn away, but reference is made to an earlier lease dated 20th December 13 Chas. I. *(L.A. DDX1423/5536/31).*

1638 – Will of Roger Kaye of Widdel, Bury *(L.A. WCW/Supra/C122B/12).* Kaye was one of the executors of the will of Henry Bury, who had left an endowment for the formation of a free school at Bury. James Walmsley was Roger Kaye's brother in law, and took over responsibility for the school money on his death.

1642 – The Protestation Returns for Turton name James *Walmesley* senior, George *Wallmsley*, James *Wallmsley* junior and Thomas *Wallmesley*, all aged eighteen or over. (P.A. HL/PO/JO/10/1/95/5).

1645 - Grant of power of attorney from James *Walmisley* of Turton, gentleman, to Thomas Holme of Rochdall [Rochdale], gentleman, to receive a debt from Humphrey Chetham of Clayton, gentleman. *(J.R.L. CLD/232).*

1647 - Indenture of lease by Humphrey Chetham to Elizabeth Walmsley, widow, concerning Siss Hey, Cocks Carr and Chapel Field, formerly in the occupation of Christopher Walmsley. For the lives of Ann Greene, wife of Richard Greene and daughter of Elizabeth Walmsley, and John Pilkington and Elizabeth Pilkington, son and daughter of Ann Greene. *(L.A. DDX1423/5536/30).*

1648 - Assignment from James *Walmisley* of Turton, gentleman, and Susan *Kaie* of Widdell in Elton, widow, to Thomas Hulme of Rochdale, gentleman, of a messuage in Turton. *(J.R.L. CLD/1182).*

1648 - Will of James Walmsley of Turton, gentleman, and proxy of renunciation. *(L.A. WCW/Supra/C145B/49 and WCW/Supra/C164B/9).*

J.R.L.   John Rylands Library
L.A.   Lancashire Archives
P.A.   Parliamentary Archives
T.N.A. The National Archives (Kew)

APPENDIX B
Inventory of the Goods & Chattels of Ralph Egerton of Turton, 1702

The original inventory also included a valuation against each item.

A true and perfect Inventory of all the Goods Chattles Cattle and Substance of Ralph Egerton Gent. Late of Turton in the Parish of Bolton in le Moors in the County of Lancaster Deceased taken and appraized by Christo. Harrocks, Jno. Taylor, Jno. Harrocks, Jno. Hampson, Thomas Anderson and Jno. Clegg the 14th day of October 1702.

Two Stewards
Item one ox
Item one Bull
Item one old Cow Called whiteface
Item one Cow called Finch
Item one Cow called Cush
Item one Cow called Hoolme
Item one Cow called Howlden
Item one Brown heifer or winter Cow
Item one Cow called Long Arse
Item one Cow called Blackburn
Item one year old Sterk
Item one Bay horse
Item one Gray horse
Item one Dunn horse
Item one Little Dun horse
Item one Black horse
Item one Gallaway
Item one Swine
Item in Corn at Lower Barn
Item in hay at Lower Barn
Item in Sives and Riddles
Item in hay at Lower Stable
Item in hay at higher Stable
Item in hay at the fould Barn
Item 2 Plowes and 2 pair of Irons
Item 2 Barrowes
Item 2 Turf Carts
Item one Clow Cart and Wheels
Item one harvest Cart and Wheels
Item 3 ox Teams

Item one Pitchfork
Item 40 Sapline Boards
Item 3 old Pack Paddles and 3 o're Lays
Item 3 Gang of [Heles?]
Item 2 old Tubs and 1 old Sledge

***In the** Garret In [S woles?]*
Item one Gt. Ark
Item one Chest
Item 2 old Coach wheels
Item one old Bedstead for firewood
Item 2 Forks spade and pitchfork
Item 2 Pitchforks in the out houseing

***In the** higher Stable*
Two Cart Saddles Carrier Crapp and Ridgwith
Item 3 pair Trase and 5 Backbands
Item 5 halters headstall and [breaning?] if they go not with horses
Item 5 Collars and 5 pair of hook [holins?]
In a place near the said stable one hemp toase
Item 3 hackney Saddles
Item Bridles for a Sled
Item one horse hilling
Item one Pillion and old Cloth
Item 2 Axes and a Pike
Item in hooks and Sickles

Item 2 Sithes and handles

In the brewhouse Three great keers
Item 6 Barrells
Item one Brew Pan
Item one Cheese Press
Item 2 Ringers and 1 Dough Beason
Item 2 Castrills and Tun Dish
Item 3 Milk and Water [Eashous?]
Item 2 Churnes
Item 1 Ironing Tubb
Item 1 Beef Tubb
Item 2 Slands
Item 2 Wood Basons
Item 3 Milk [Gullins?]
Item 6 Milk Troughs
Item 5 Charpotts
Item 1 Swine Tubb
Item 5 Cans

In the Parlour in whitewood back
stools
Item one Couch Chair
Item one Square Table
Item one Sett work Carpett
Item one Little table
Item one other Sett work Carpet on it
Item one Childer Chair
Item one Large Looking Glass
Item 2 Coats of Arms
Item 7 Pictures very old not valued
Item fire shovell Tongs and Grate

In the Hall one old Long Table
Item one Chest of Drawers
Item one old Clock and Bell
Item 3 Green Back stools
Item 1 Little Brandy Seller
Item 1 old Livery Table
Item 1 fire Iron and Tongs
Item 1 old hour Glass and Frame
Item 1 old Chair

*[4 lines giving weights of brass and
pewter pots etc.]*

In the green Chamber
one bedsted Matt and cord Curtains
vallans head Cloth and Teaster
Item 1 feather bed and Bolster at 3d lb
Item 1 Large Arm'd Chair
Item 1 Green Back Stool
Item 1 Small Square Table
Item 1 Chest of Drawers
Item 1 Desk
Item 1 Press
*Item 3 Pictures belonged to the
Familly at Shaw as was said*
Item 1 Iron grate wth Brass Bolls
Item Brass Land Irons

In the Buttery one old Square Cofferr
Item one Large Cofferr
Item 1 Little Cofferr
Item in the near Buttery one Cupboard
Item 4 Doz of Trenchers
Item 1 Square Table
Item 1 Standing Cupboard
Item 1 Stand

In the kitchen
Two fouling Pieces and 2 Muskets
Item 1 Square Table and 3 Formes
Item 1 Warming Pan
Item 1 Jack
Item 1 Salt Chest
Item 3 Whitewood Chairs
Item 4 Spitts
Item apair of Gorbutts
Item 3 hacking knives
Item 1 Cleever
*Item 1 Fix Iron Shovell Tongs and 2
Crows*
Item 1 Smoothing Iron and heater
Item 1 Salt Box
Item 1 Frying pan

Item 2 Chafeing Dishes
Item 2 Dripping Pans
Item 1 Joint Stool
Item 1 Iron Bradreth
Item 3 hung shelves
Item 1 Cockle Pan
Item 1 Brass Pott Boyler
Item 1 Iron Pott
Item 2 old Pans and an old Shellet
Item 1 Iron Back spittle

In the Dairy
one old Long Table
Item 1 whitewood Chair
Item 1 Tresl
Item 7 Whitewood Shelves
Item 2 Corn Baggs
Item 5 Sacks
Item 2 Small Baggs
Item in Earthen ware
Item 6 Butter Muggs

In the Larder one cupboard
Item 1 old Cofferr
Item 1 Still and bottom

In the Brewhouse Chamber
1 Gt. Ark with feathers in it
Item 1 Meal ark
Item 1 Long Cofferr
Item 1 Strike
Item 1 pair of Whitewood Bedstock
Item 1 feather bed Bolster and Pillows
Item 2 Blanketts and an old Rugg
Item 1 other Bedstead
Item 1 Chaffe Bed feather Bolster and
Pillows
Item 3 old Blanketts
Item 1 pair of Weights
Item 1 Cart Reap and an old Chair

In the white Chamber
one old bedstead with sacking bottom
and chair covers and Sawed Curtains
wth Suner Curtains & Vallans
Item 1 feather Bed and Bolsers and a
pillow
Item 1 pair of Blankets and
Counterpane
Item 7 old backstools and 3 joint
Stools
Item 1 Chest of Drawers
Item 1 Looking Glass
Item 1 Close Stool Case
Item 2 Window Curtains
Item in the Passage 1 Little Press

In the Little Stairhead Chamber
Two Steeled Steads
Item 1 old Blanket
Item 2 old Chairs

In the Porch Chamber
one bedstead Matt and Cord Curtains
Vallans and Counterpane
Item 1 feather bed 1 Bolster 5 Pillows
Item 1 Pair of Blanketts
Item 1 Callicoe Quilt
Item 1 Square Table
Item 1 Looking Glass with Brass
hooks
Item 3 Stools
Item in White Mettall Potts and
Glasses
Item 4 Doz of Glass Bottles

In the Closet
One Oak box with Drawers in it
Item 1 Square Table
Item 1 old Cupboard
Item 2 Fustian Ends
Item 1 Whitewood Box and a small
Box
Item 3 Small boxes more

Item in Flax
Item in Round Yarn
Item 10lb in Flaxen Yarn
Item 1 Desk
Item 1 Little Cupboard

In the *Spout Chamber*
One Bedstead Matt and Cord
Item 1 feather Bed and Bolster
Item 1 White Blanket
Item 1 Yellow Blanket
Item 1 Little Bedstead Matt and Cord
Item 1 feather Bed and Bolster
Item 1 Pair of Blanketts
Item Chest of Drawers
Item 4 old Trunkes
Item 1 Joint Stool
Item 2 old Curtains and vallans
Item 3 Whitewood boxes

In the *Porch Chamber one box and old Trunk*

In the *Little Room at Stair head one Bedstead Mat and Cord*
Item 1 feather Bed Bolster & Pillows
Item 2 old Blankets

In Linnen

[59 lines omitted here; towels, tablecloths, napkins, blankets etc.]

Item 14 Gold Rings - One Signet Ring, 4 Stone Rings, Nine Plain Rings
Item 3 Silver Boxes and Silver Buttons
Item 6 Silver Spoons
Item 1 Gt. Silver Salt
Item 1 Little Silver Salt
Item 1 Silver Tumbler
Item 15 part of Clasps and a Tabler
Item 4 Gt. Silver Tankard
Item 1 Pocket Watch

In the *Kitchen Chamber*
One bedstead Mat Cord Curtains & vallans
Item 1 heather bed and 2 Bolster
Item 1 pair of Blanketts
Item 1 Counterpane
Item 1 Window Curtain
Item 1 Looking Glass
Item 3 old black stools and a joint stool
Item 1 Iron Grate fire shovell and Tongs
Item 1 Portmantua Trunk
Item 2 old Boxes
Item 5oz of Burnt Silver
Item in Purse and apparell
Item in Butter and Cheese left at Turton when broke up house

Total value £205:08:03½

APPENDIX C
1787 List of Objectors - Proposed Turnpike Road

List of people who objected to the proposed Blackburn & Bolton turnpike road, at a general meeting of the principal landowners and inhabitants of Turton on September 11th 1787.

1. Amos Ogden *
2. Jno. Brandwood *
3. Samuel Hall
4. Thomas Smith *
5. James Lomax *
6. Edmd. Haworthe *
7. John Ormrod *
8. Thos. Bridge
9. John Crook
10. James Mason
11. Geo. Holme
12. John Entwisle *
13. John Haworth *
14. Edmund Wood
15. Thos. Wood *
16. George Holt
17. John Haslam
18. James Haworthe *
19. Thomas Mason
20. John Wood *
21. Roger Hamer
22. John Dewhurst

23. Thomas Kershaw
24. Saml. Knowles *
25. Richard Thomason
26. Richard Orrell *
27. John Mason
28. Jas. Knowles
29. William Holt
30. John Knowles
31. John Orrell
32. Isaac Orrell
33. John Hardman
34. Joseph Walch
35. John Crook (Matherfold)
36. Roger Ratcliff
37. James Pilling
38. Wm. Walch
39. Adam Lomax
40. William Haslam
41. George Warburton
42. James Warburton
43. Giles Marsh
44. Jeremiah Marsh

* Subsequently became trustees of the 1797 Bolton & Blackburn turnpike road.

APPENDIX D

1836 Electoral Register – Egerton, Dunscar & Dimple

Name	*Place of Abode*	*Property or Tenant*
Ashworth, Edmund	Egerton hall, Turton	William Dearden, tenant
Barry, James	Chorley new road, Lt. Bolton	Barry Row
Bridge, John	Rock, Turton	Rock
Bentley, Lawrence	Cross guns, Turton	Cross guns
Crook, William	Mather fold, Turton	Mather fold farm
Crook, Peter	Whittle's, Turton	Whittles farm
Cristy, Thomas	Broomfield, Essex	Bedford row
Dearden, William	Egerton, Turton	Egerton farm
Edge, Robert	Globe inn, Turton	Self occupier
Gill, Joseph	Dewhurst's, Turton	Self occupier
Hemer, John	Volunteer, Turton	Dunscar gate
Haworth, Adam L.	Higher Dunscar, Turton	Self occupier
Horrocks, Thomas	Stones, Turton	Stones
Horrocks, Helm	Stanrose, Turton	Stones
Horrocks, Edmund	Stanrose, Turton	Stanrose
Hoare, Richard Peter	Southfield, Somersetshire	Cockscar
Hamer, Benjamin	Cross guns, Turton	Cross guns
Kay, Richard	Buff's, Turton	Dimple Row and Cock hall
Kay, John	Buff's, Turton	Dimple Row and Cock hall
Kay, Richard, sen.	Dimple Row, Turton	Dimple Row
Kenyon, William	Stones, Turton	Stones
Kay, Richard, jun.	Dimple, Turton	Dimple
Marsh, James	Parrs, Turton	Cock hall
Martland, Richard	James street, Blackburn	Cross guns
Orrell, John	Haworth's, Turton	Haworths
Probert, William	Eagley school	Dimple
Ratcliffe, John	Stanrose, Turton	Stanrose
Slater, George	Dunscar, Turton	Dunscar farm
Slater, James	Dunscar, Turton	Dunscar farm
Smith, William	Pillings, Turton	Stanrose
Smith, Richard	Sharrocks, Turton	Stones
Taylor, John	Stones, Turton	Stones
Warburton, James	Stones, Turton	Stones
Warbutton, George	Old school, Turton	Old school